D1234078

Latino Communities

Emerging Voices

Political, Social, Cultural, and Legal Issues

Edited by
Antoinette Sedillo Lopez
University of New Mexico

A ROUTLEDGE SERIES

LATINO COMMUNITIES: EMERGING VOICES

Antoinette Sedillo Lopez, *General Editor*

THE QUEST FOR TEJANO IDENTITY IN SAN ANTONIO, TEXAS, 1913–2000

Richard A. Buitron, Jr.

ROUTLEDGE
New York & London

Published in 2004 by
Routledge
270 Madison Avenue
New York, NY 10016
www.routledge-ny.com

Published in Great Britain by
Routledge
2 Park Square
Milton Park, Abingdon,
Oxon OX14 4RN
www.routledge.co.uk

Routledge is an imprint of the Taylor and Francis Group.

Copyright © 2004 Routledge

Library of Congress Cataloging-In-Publication data

Buitron, Richard A., 1961-
  The quest for Tejano identity in San Antonio, Texas, 1913–2000 / by Richard A. Buitron, Jr.
     p. cm.
  Includes bibliographical references and index.
  ISBN 0-415-94950-5 (hardback : alk. paper)
  1. Mexican Americans—Ethnic identity—Texas—San Antonio. 2. Mexican Americans—Texas—San Antonio—Social conditions—20th century. 3. Mexican Americans—Texas—San Antonio—Intellectual life—20th century. 4. Community life—Texas—San Antonio—History—20th century. 5. San Antonio (Tex.)—Social conditions—20th century. 6. San Antonio (Tex.)—Ethnic relations. 7. San Antonio (Tex.)—Intellectual life—20th century. 8. Mexican Americans—California—Los Angeles—Social conditions—20th century. 9. Los Angeles (Calif.)—Ethnic relations. I. Title.
  F394.S2119M5135 2004
  976.4'3510046872073—dc22   2004005110

DEDICATED to my mother,
Rose Hernandez Buitron, 1929–1999,
who taught me that history can give us
significance.

Contents

Preface

WPA writers trying to capture the essence of the Texan city of San Antonio quoted a Spanish legend saying that he "who drinks at San Antonio's river once, will drink of it again."[1] Since Mexicans established the first missions in the early eighteenth century, San Antonio has retained its original flavor as a former outpost in the Spanish Empire. After Texas became a republic, and later part of the United States, San Antonio's original population became an ostracized minority. Yet even as an Anglo-American city, San Antonio remained tied to its Mexican history. Even the siege of the Alamo, the city's defining event, was connected simultaneously to its colonial, Mexican and American legacies. As San Antonio has changed and grown, its residents of Mexican descent, the *Tejanos*, have struggled to establish their identity. Like their city, they were at once a Mexican people and an American people.

The initial stage of Mexican-American historical interpretation began when the editor of the liberal journal *The Nation*, Carey McWilliams, discussed his observations about the Mexican-American community in *North from Mexico*, the first in a new tradition of Chicano historical scholarship.[2] McWilliams believed that Mexican Americans were unique among ethnic groups and were not treated as other European immigrants, socially, politically or historically. His thesis was emulated by later Chicano historians such as Rodolfo Acuña.[3]

The internal colonial model was first conceived by African American sociologist Robert Blauner and was frequently used by Chicano historians in describing their situation in the U.S. It asserts that people of color were deliberately and permanently assigned a marginal role in the U.S. by white Americans, designated to be only a menial labor force. In such a scheme, Mexican Americans never would be truly Americans, but exist in a quasi-national status, not unlike citizens in Third World countries. The internal colonial model only partially explains the history of Texans of

Mexican heritage. George J. Sanchez and Juan Gomez-Quiñones both believed that internal colonialism does not account for the variation of experience between Mexican Americans of different communities and at various points in history.[4] This study bears out their thesis. The internal colonial model also casts Latinos as victims, and excludes their agency in their history.

Inspired by the Civil Rights movement and the resulting Chicano Studies movement, scholars began to reexamine the history of San Antonio in light of the question of Tejano identity in the 1980s. Jesus de la Teja, Gerald Poyo, Gilberto Hinojosa,[5] and Timothy Matovina, with his book *Tejano Religion and Ethnicity*[6] have all studied the early history of San Antonio and the development of its culture. David Montejano's book *Anglos and Mexicans in the Making of Texas*[7] was a social history focusing on the condition of rural Tejanos in the deep south of Texas.

The literature regarding immigrant communities in the American urban setting is extensive and growing. The critical place of San Antonio in the development of modern Tejano thinking was most clearly revealed by the works of historians Richard A. Garcia, Mario Garcia and Cynthia Orozco.[8] Their writings include *The Rise of the Mexican American Middle Class, San Antonio 1929–41*, by Richard A. Garcia, *Mexican Americans: Leadership, Ideology and Identity, 1930–1960* by Mario T. Garcia and "The Origins of the League of United Latin American Citizens (LULAC) and the Mexican American Civil Rights Movement in Texas, With an Analysis of the Political Participation of Women in a Gendered Context" by Orozco.

Richard Garcia's work is an in-depth look at the social, religious, political, and intellectual forces in San Antonio that were at work in the creation of what he called the "Mexican American mind," that sense of identity forged among primarily middle-class, native born citizens of Mexican descent that was the seed bed of political activism in the post World War II era. The focus of the Mexican-American generation had moved from Mexico to the United States. This was in contrast to members of the Mexican revolutionary exile group, with whom the Mexican Americans were chronological contemporaries.

Mario Garcia took a generational approach in comprehending the development of Mexican-American thought in the U.S. Elaborating, the author declared, "the Mexican American Era is set apart, on the one hand, from the Immigrant Era with its stress on the politics of immigration and, on the other, from the seceding and separationist-oriented Chicano Movement of the 1960s."[9] Garcia's method reveals the heterogeneity of the Mexican-American community across both generational, class, and geographic boundaries.

Cynthia Orozco at UCLA also researched the origins of the Mexican-American mentality. Her dissertation argued that the development of Richard Garcia's "Mexican American mind" actually began in the twenties with the organization of groups like the Order Sons of America and after the crisis of identity that took place at the Harlingen convention of 1927. At this convention of advocacy groups, Mexican-American leaders made the fateful decision to exclude Mexican citizens from the civil rights body that ultimately became LULAC, declaring themselves Americans. Like Richard Garcia, Orozco found that two primary causes created the ideology formed by LULAC and groups like them. The first of these was in the social and political environment of government, church, family and school in South Texas. The second catalyst was the push of historical forces on the region, namely the advent of mass transportation and national capitalist market, the Mexican Revolution and the two World Wars.

Thirdly, George J. Sanchez's *Becoming Mexican American*[10] denied the asserted cultural polarities of Chicano scholarship and offered a postmodern model, where both American and Mexican cultures are in a constant state of change. His literary counterpart is novelist Sandra Cisneros from San Antonio, whose novels and short stories gave voice to the experiences of the urban Mexican-American woman.

It is a matter of great controversy both outside and inside the Mexican-American community as to whether their ethnic experience had a different intellectual impact than immigrants from Europe. American society was much slower in receiving Mexican Americans into the cultural mainstream than they were with the Germans, Italians, or the Irish. Also, discrimination against Mexicans has been more sustained, built into the customs and structures of Southwestern culture, and was often more violent. In short, the difference between the treatment of Mexicans and Europeans was in how earlier Americans received the two immigrant groups.

I agree with Richard Garcia that the search for a collective historical consciousness has been a central intellectual project of Mexican Americans. Writers of the Spanish-language newspaper *La Prensa* during the 1910s and 1920s, the League of United Latin American Citizens during and after the 1930s, and Chicano movement activists in the sixties and seventies all desired to construct an identity for the Mexican-descent population of San Antonio. What Garcia and others have not explored is how Mexicans have appropriated various intellectual traditions to form their consciousness, and the events that caused them to choose as they did.

Scholars such as Thomas Bender have discussed the role that the social, regional, and even architectural shape of a city can play in influencing the views and opinions of its intellectual community. Regarding Mexican Americans, this facet of the life of the urban mind has been explored by Richard Garcia, George J. Sanchez in his study of Los Angeles Chicanos, and Richard Griswold del Castillo in his comparisons of California and Texas.

Regional and local histories have had a profound impact in creating a distinctive ethnic community among Mexican Americans in San Antonio. The chief of these distinctions is a historical narrative grounded in the

Mexican, frontier, and southern experiences, and forms an identity set apart from other Mexican-American communities. In this environment, a number of groups attempted to create a global identity based on either American or Mexican experiences. While each of these (the pan-Mexican vision of *La Prensa*, the pluralistic vision of the middle class, and the nationalistic paradigm of Chicanos) was compelling, none really succeeded in creating a Mexican-American identity that captured the entire community.

Also, the historical distinctiveness of communities such as San Antonio is being mitigated by two factors. Improvements in communication and travel during the last sixty years caused a globalization of Spanish-speaking citizens throughout the U.S. and with Americans of other backgrounds. Second, the increasing autonomy of the individual American from community institutions makes the maintenance of local, ethnic, and national identities extremely difficult. The ahistorical nature of individualism works against the coherence of a collective identity.

This study emphasizes the centrality of the historical narrative in the creation and development of identity. At a time when the discipline of history is being marginalized in the academic realm, it is hoped that this study can begin to reaffirm history's relevance.

Acknowledgments

Many thanks to those who helped bring this work to completion. To Dr. Neil Jumonville, my major professor, for his direction, patience and encouragement as we communicated across the country. For Debbie Perry, graduate advisor at Florida State University Department of History, who is indispensable to all graduates in keeping track of our deadlines.

Appreciation must also go out to all those who contributed their wealth of experience and memory through their interviews, including the late judge Carlos Cadena, who spoke to me of his friendship with Henry B. Gonzalez and Gus Garcia. Thanks also to Congressman Charles Gonzalez for the invaluable information about his father. Ruben Mungia, for his interview regarding his family history, his life, the life of the West Side of San Antonio, and for all the primary material that allowed this study to come to life. Gratitude also to Dr. Felix Almaráz, who shared with me his biography of Carlos Castañeda, and who was supportive throughout. To Beatriz Gallego, founding member of COPS for her impressions on its history. Thanks also to her daughter Annette, who introduced me to her mother and the historical smorgasbord that was her studio! For his thoughts and memories of Chicano art in San Antonio, *gracias* to David Gonzales of the Guadalupe Cultural Arts Center. Finally, for Sandra Cisneros, who took time out of her busy schedule for our interview. It was great spending time with another former Chicagoan.

I must also mention the several libraries and their staffs who assisted my research. The libraries of Florida State University; the Benson Latin American Collection and the Center for American History of the University of Texas at Austin, with their extensive collections of *La Prensa* and *LULAC News*, were of immense help. The libraries of the University of Texas at San Antonio, St. Mary's University and its law school, Texas

A&M University at Kingsville, and the San Antonio Public Library, most especially its Texana collection, gave assistance as well.

For their love, prayers and humor, a word of gratitude for my home congregations: First Christian Church of Tallahassee, Coastal Bend Fellowship of Kingsville, Texas, and the Alamo City Christian Fellowship of San Antonio.

Chapter One

Formation of Community, 1519–1910

In contemplating his people, the Mexican Octavio Pàz observed, "The history of Mexico is the history of a man seeking his parentage, his origins."[1] Coming to an understanding of their identity was and remains the great struggle of the Mexican, both those in Mexico and even more for those who are citizens of the United States. That identity is founded in a four-hundred-year-old Mexican culture grounded in external authority through both its American and European origins. Identity was based on the feudal paradigm of the land, tradition, religion (whether that religion was based in organizations like the church or in folk practices), and the family. This dependence on external authority had a much greater hold in Latin America than in the north, and became a distinguishing factor in the whole history of Mexican-American thought.

In 1691 Spanish soldiers and clerics brought this culture to a Native American settlement known as Yanaguana, but named by the newcomers as San Antonio de Bexar.[2] Due to the springs that formed the source of the San Antonio River, the area was an oasis in a semi-arid region, and became an outpost of the Spanish Empire in 1719. Ultimately, its residents, though heirs of the Mexican identity, created their own unique expression, one that distinguished them from other parts of the Empire's far north, today's American Southwest. As noted by Jesus de la Teja, San Antonio's isolation created a spirit of independence among its inhabitants.[3] Its interaction with Anglo American culture after 1821 (the year of Mexican independence) and the influx of revolutionary exiles after 1913 all combined to produce a mind which was both Mexican and American. Politically, this ideology was centered on the personal, yet relied on the existing system; it valued deference and tradition, yet exalted progress and equality; and it used social protest, not revolution as a means of change. These factors of geography, cultural interaction, economics and religion produced a unique Tejano identity whose independence, both from mainstream American thought and of Mexican-American communities elsewhere, has continued to the present.

An awareness of the development of Mexican-American identity can be gained by examining the traditions of Tejano thought and culture through the lens of some of its representative thinkers. Our aim will be to take small slices out of the Mexican-American tradition and examine generalists who commented on the assumptions of their day.

THE PRE-COLUMBIAN TRADITION:
THE FLORENTINE CODEX

Anthropologist John Bierhorst discovered that sixty-two years before Columbus, the Aztec rulers of Mexico destroyed the histories of earlier cultures that were derogatory to them.[4] The Mexican conception of identity has therefore been in a state of flux from its very beginning. The first Europeans who met them found a society that was very nearly the equal of their own. For nearly eighteen centuries the indigenous peoples of Mexico had lived in an organized, agriculturally-based civilization. Legend held that the Mexica (Mesheeka) or Aztec peoples had journeyed from a region called Aztlán, an area somewhere in the northern desert of Mexico; most likely they were nomads from that region around the thirteenth century. By 1500 they dominated Mexico's central valley and gave their name to the region and nation. Borrowing much of their civilization from earlier tribes, the Mexica built cities with populations in the thousands and a hierarchical religion and government. They had inherited from earlier cultures an alphabet and produced a voluminous body of literature in books called *codices*. Unveiled by Mexica writing is an educated and scholarly people. A student of Aztec codex writing observed, "[The *Codex Mendoza*] includes scenes showing parents educating their children; others showing the education of youngsters in public schools . . . Education is a recurring theme, the noble arts and professions are discussed at length."[5]

At the time of the Spanish conquest in 1520, Mexica writers had accumulated an extensive codex library. Most of this collection was destroyed during the Spanish conquest and only a few have made it to the present, the most important of which is the *Florentine Codex*.[6] The codex was compiled after the conquest by Spanish monk Bernardino de Sahagún (d.1590). The Florentine Codex was an assemblage of Mexica culture, religion, folkways, and politics.[7] It is from this work and the few remaining like it that an understanding of the mind and life of the peoples of Mexico can be gained. The codex revealed that Mexica society, like Europe in the Middle Ages, contained religious persons who also functioned as the culture's poets and intellectuals.[8] Sahagún's compilation also revealed Mexica thinking with regard to the universe and their place in it. Referring to their gods, passages such as these were typical: "our lord of the near, lord of the nigh, is made to laugh. He is arbitrary, he is capricious, he mocketh. He willeth in the manner he desireth." Humanity was perceived as dice in the hands of deity; "He is placing us in the palm of his hand; he is making us round. We roll; we become as pellets. He is casting us from side to side. We make him laugh; he is making a mockery of us."[9]

In contrast to the Enlightenment conception of an understandable and partially controllable universe, Mexicas saw their world as mysterious and out of their power. The impact of this view upon the Mexican perception was that "Reality exists by itself here, has a life of its own," wrote Octavio Páz, "and was not invented by man as it was in the United States."[10] This fatalism created a literary and psychological trait of self-depreciation that was viewed by Páz as a perception of inferiority that would have a profound influence on Mexican and Chicano culture.[11]

With an outlook so similar to the philosophy of predestination prevalent in Calvinist Europe, the Mexica saw themselves as people of destiny and understood the successes and failures of life as transitory. A nation or person might be favored by the gods one moment and discarded later. Individual humans were important only as they submitted to their designated place in the culture.[12] Mexica writings reveal a hierarchical yet interdependent society, where all roles were valued. Like frontier America in Alexis de Tocqueville's writings, adherence to traditional roles for men and women was enforced more by cultural peer pressure than by submission to political and religious authorities, who were also to comply with a designated code of behavior and responsibility.

Aztec cosmology would be both their greatest strength and their greatest weakness. With it the Aztecs carved out cities in the Valley of Mexico and conquered a vast empire. In their minds, it was part of the natural order of things that they should dominate their world. However, that same sense of destiny proved to be their undoing. According to Mexica mythology, there was also a time appointed when the world as they knew it would end, when "white gods" would come and rule over them. That time was the spring of 1519, at precisely the time that Hernan Cortés and his small band of soldiers arrived on the shores of Veracruz.

SPANISH THOUGHT IN THE NEW WORLD: ALVA AND DE LA CRUZ

Cortés and the other Spanish conquerors arrived in Mexico with a tradition of martial valor forged in the Crusades, the decades' long Reconquest of Spain from the Moslem Moors, and most recently the religious movement of the Counterreformation. According to Manuel Orozco y Berra, this glorification of conquest and new sense of opportunity and freedom combined to accentuate what became the character of the Spaniard in Mexico, with all its many contradictions: "Loyal to their king, valiant and spirited; tenacious and religious to the point of superstition; confident and arrogant; cruel to the conquered because they were of a despised race; implacable in the persecution of idolaters; rapacious to make their fortune, prodigal in wasting it at the gaming table or on pleasures once it was won; fervent preachers and corrupt soldiers."[13]

The Spanish were part of larger ideological and economic trends at the time. The first trend was the competition and expansion of Protestantism and Catholicism in Europe and throughout the world. Manuel Gonzales argued that "From a historical perspective, the power of religious faith, especially during the Age of Reformation, should not be underestimated," and pointed out that, "[s]o convinced were the missionaries in the righteousness of their cause that many were willing to risk martyrdom to spread the holy faith."[14]

Also, Europeans began to seek economic and political opportunity outside of Europe and the confines of the medieval, feudal system. In the New World the conquistador found himself liberated from the strict conventions of Spanish culture, most particularly the economic strictures imposed by the system of primogeniture. These trends produced in nations as diverse as Spain and England the ideal of mission as central to the national identity. For the Spanish this mission was the conversion of the Indians to Catholicism and the exploitation of their wealth for the glory of Spain.

Interaction between European and non-European peoples began their long and tortured history in the colony of New Spain, commencing with the conquests of Cortés in 1520.[15] Along with disease (which killed millions) the process of intermarriage produced an entirely new race of mestizos, persons of mixed Spanish and Indian heritage who became the dominant group and created, in effect, an entirely new nation. "The growing mexicano culture and identity," Juan Gomez-Quioñes elaborated, "with particular regional variations, was dominant over the local indigenous peoples, who were largely amalgamated through forced Mexicanization."[16] On the other hand, Manuel Gonzales believed that through its language and culture Mexico "became more Spanish than Spain itself."[17]

Nowhere was this amalgamation of the races more evident than in the writings of Fernando de Alva Ixtlilxochitl, (1580–1648) a Hispanized Mexica who became renowned for his histories of the Pre-Columbian and colonial eras. But as Gomez-Quiñones astutely observed, de Alva's work was wrought with a particular tension. "The writings of Fernando de Alba [sic] Ixtlilxochitl represent the work of the indio-mestizo driven by the urge to inform the world of the glories of ancient Mexico with which he identified. But he also was at war with himself in . . . simultaneously claiming credit for the conquest by highlighting Indian contributions to it."[18] De Alva was the descendent of Ixtlilxochitl, the king of Texcoco, a vassal city-state of the Aztecs. Resentful of Aztec rule, the elder Ixtlilxochitl became the leader of rebellious native tribes, without which Cortés and his 500 Spaniards would have been unable to take control of the immense empire. De Alva believed his mission as a historian was "to write the history of the lords of the land, especially of Don Fernando Ixtlilxochitl and his brothers and relatives, because their heroic deeds are buried, and there is no one who remembers them and the help which they gave to the Spaniards."[19] His writings show that internal rivalries were as much to blame for the downfall of the Mexicas as was the treachery and rapaciousness of the Spaniard, and challenge the paradigm of victimization commonly employed in the history of the Spanish conquest. De Alva's history reveals that the creation of present-day Mexican society was a mixture of cooperation and conflict, as was the case throughout the New World. Second, by so self-consciously seeking to preserve a threatened history, de Alva shared with Cotton Mather of New England a sense of the importance of history to preserving one's historical identity. Both may have intuitively sensed that without an internalized set of values laid down by ancestors, one could be too easily molded by external forces, whether those were increasing assimilation with Spanish culture, or increasing secularism.

Most importantly, it is in the work of de Alva that we begin to see the ambiguity present in the Mexican identity, an identity torn between the values of the indigenous American and the Spaniard. The identity of the mestizo, and of all Mexicans, was muddied by simultaneous conflict and mixture of cultures. During the colonial era and for centuries afterward, status in Mexican society was determined by racial ancestry. People of Indian and mixed race were placed in a lesser rank, excluded from political power. This racial discrimination had a profound psychological effect on the nation as a whole. "The Mexican," writer Samuel Ramos postulated, "finds himself in the middle, and to be there is his destiny, for he is not really American [Indian] and no longer Spanish. Thus the Mexican, the compulsive imitator, considers himself an inferior being."[20] Páz described the history of the Mexican as a tragic quest for a lost parentage, who desired "to go back beyond the catastrophe he suffered . . . to be a sun again, to return to the center of that life from which he was separated."[21] Just as the black thinkers like Langston Hughes and James Baldwin sought an identity which was not African but yet not white American, Mexicans and their descendants in the United States would be forced to grapple with the same critical issue.

De Alva followed in a train of writers and other advocates of Mexica autonomy. Bernardino de Sahagún expressed admiration rather than scorn for much of Aztec culture and sought to preserve it through his voluminous and detailed writings, becoming one of modern history's first anthropologists. Another Spanish cleric, Bartolome de las Casas, recorded the atrocities suffered by native Americans. By resorting to religious and secular authority (scripture, pronouncements of Pope and King) in a largely unsuccessful battle to defend Indian rights, Las Casas mirrored contemporary Protestant Reformers, in particular the New England Puritans. Through his debates, treatises and books, de las Casas stood in a long tradition of prophetic voices by relying on external authority to conform others to a standard of righteousness.

Colonial Mexico's other outstanding intellectual was Sor Juana Inés de la Cruz (1648–1695), a Catholic nun recognized in her day as a writer and thinker of remarkable genius. That talent was hindered, however, by the status of women in colonial Mexican society. Denied a mainstream education, de la Cruz entered a convent in order to follow her literary and intellectual pursuits. Four years before her death, de la Cruz defended the intellectual capabilities of women and her own right to be a scholar, which her superiors contested. Citing a list of women in biblical, classical, and European history, Juana concluded, "a great throng of women . . . all were nothing more than learned women, held, and celebrated–and venerated as well–as such by antiquity."[22] Because these women were held in high esteem in their time, de la Cruz felt that attempts to prevent her from writing and studying were unjustified. de la Cruz was the contemporary of other important female thinkers such as Anne Bradstreet, Anne Hutchison, and Mary Wollstonecraft, all of whom desired to enter intellectual realms formerly reserved for men.

The expressions of de la Cruz were wide-ranging, encompassing poetry, fiction, and nonfiction, and even drama written in three languages: Spanish, Latin, and the Mexica tongue of Nahuatl. Her interests included the religious, secular, and even the scientific. Such was her intellect that her musings on the subject of beauty would be comparable to those of Jonathan Edwards a half-century later.

"[de la Cruz'] theology of beauty" George H. Tavard summarized, "turns around three related concepts. First, there is the understanding of beauty itself. Second, since beauty seen in a theological perspective, is spiritual, even when also physical, there is a certain understanding of what constitutes the relation between beauty and grace; for Juana Inés de la Cruz, this relation is identical with love. Third, there is a global perception of what beauty ultimately reveals, namely the glory of God, manifested in his creation."[23]

Because of the feudal aspects in the Spanish and Mexica culture, individuals in Mexican society in large measure were significant only in terms of their contribution to the family, religion or societal tradition. This would have important consequences for the formation of the Mexican-American mind. It also made reforms of any kind very difficult, since the status quo was highly valued. The life and work of Sor Juana Inés de la Cruz is one example of this trend. The religious hierarchy of Mexico believed that her status as a woman dictated that she confine her intellectual activities to religious topics. Another example of the power of feudal institutions in Mexico was the difficulties encountered by Mexican advocates of independence from Spain.

MEXICO'S EARLY REPUBLIC, 1821–1846

The impulses behind nearly all of the independence movements in Latin America were a growing desire for home rule and self-determination among local elites and a desire by those same elites to maintain the social and political structures of Spain. The character of these revolutions thus became elitist, nationalist, and conservative. Mexico was no exemption to this rule, where it was conservatives, not liberals, who successfully created a new state.

Mexico's political position of total subservience relative to Spain was formed during a three-hundred-year colonial history. Complete control was exerted by the mother country in church, state, and most of the economy. Simon Bolivar, the nineteenth century revolutionary of South America, decried a condition of what he called "political infancy." In elaborating, he said that "if we could at least have managed our domestic affairs and internal administration, we could have acquainted ourselves with the process and mechanics of public affairs."[24] Spain's strict mercantile philosophy viewed all its colonies in Latin America as appendages of the domestic economy. Additionally, all major offices in the Catholic Church in Mexico were held exclusively by Spaniards. The result was that the entire local population of Mexico—Creole, mestizo, and Native American—were almost entirely excluded from the governance of New Spain.

At the beginning of the nineteenth century, a community of Mexican writers and commentators known as the Guadalupes attempted to change this situation and create an independent and liberal Mexican state. The Guadalupes (who named themselves for the patron saint of indigenous Mexico, the Virgin of Guadalupe)[25] were a group of Mexican liberals composed of clergy and laymen who were consistently imbibing the liberal thought of England, the United States, and France. From their study of this ideology the Guadalupes became advocates of an end to feudal privilege, the separation of church and state, and most importantly, the independence of Mexico from Spain. The main vehicle of their advocacy was the printed word, especially in newspapers and in letters to the Spanish viceroy. Forced to take a collective pseudonym out of fear of colonial persecution, the Guadalupes became one of Mexico's first communities of political discourse, like a similar liberal community in England during the early eighteenth century. Intellectuals such as John Trenchard (1662–1723), Thomas Gordon (d.1750), and English Whigs created a republican ideology that later became the unifying force in the American colonies' drive for independence.[26]

The Guadalupes and other activists for Mexican independence were at the height of their influence at a time when traditional Spanish culture was being challenged both internally and externally after the overthrow of the Spanish monarchy by Napoleon Bonaparte in 1808. Liberals desired to implement their ideals throughout the Hispanic world. A more lenient colonial government permitted the Guadalupes to begin a discussion of political issues and Mexican independence. The crowning achievement of the Guadalupes was the election in 1812 of Mexican representatives to the Spanish parliament, or Cortes, who favored Mexican independence. This brief victory was erased when the Spanish monarch dissolved the Cortes a year later and resumed absolutist rule, with a corresponding crackdown on the Mexican activists. The Guadalupes faced another handicap in advocating an ideology that was foreign to many Mexicans. Liberalism was the direct product of the historical experience of British and Americans, whereas Mexicans could only borrow a foreign ideology.

After independence in 1821, the continued division between the educated, liberal European elite and the mass of the Mexican population became a fatal flaw in that nation's political system. While the American Revolution was also led by Creole elite, its rhetoric and ideals expressed a consensus held by much of United States society. This was not the case in Mexico, where a two-tiered culture produced a corrupt and divided ruling class. Gomez-Quiñones observed that the Mexican elite were riven by a number of important issues. Commenting on the lack of political cohesion along Mexico's northern border, he declared that "both liberalism and federalism *vis-à-vis* centralism and conservative rule" vied for the allegiance of the Mexican population.[27] In the United States, debate regarding the desirability of a centralized or decentralized government took place within an overall belief in the Constitution and a supporting liberal ideology. Callcott observed that even the country's origins seemed to dictate against a federal regime: "The [Mexican] Federalists, carried away by the success . . . of the United States as a federal republic, did not realize that in the northern neighbor's territory the union of the thirteen states . . . had arisen out of decentralization, whereas in Mexico the reverse was true; decentralization was to follow unity."[28]

Also, there was no common ground regarding how to solve Mexico's internal and external problems. Gomez-Quiñones saw that on a whole host of issues, members of Mexico's elite were at loggerheads. These included the questions of federalism and centralism, education, the government's relationship to the military and the Catholic Church, even the crucial problem of identity (liberals idealizing an indigenous Aztec past, while conservatives romanticized the colonial Spanish history).[29] Finally, the conditions that cause a liberal society to flourish (a strong middle class) were not yet present in Mexico. The economy was still based on a feudalistic system of large landholdings, and the Catholic Church was strongly supported by the state. Mexican liberals, though articulate, were never a majority of the elite. This created political instability and the eventual overthrow of constitutional institutions in favor of military dictatorship in 1835. The struggle between the liberal and conservative ideals created a national weakness that was in part responsible for the ease with which Anglo-Americans took parts of northern Mexico, today's Southwestern United States.

To summarize, the micromanagement of Mexican colonial affairs by Spain hampered the implementation of an indigenous liberal ideology. The immediate effect was that with the arrival of independence in 1822, Mexico had no heritage of participatory government comparable to the United States. The other factor impeding the development of liberal thought was the stratified nature of Mexican society, in which the community of discourse was composed of only a small elite class. Finally, Mexican thought until

1846 was divided by competing historiographies that arose out of the ambiguity of Mexican identity. Mexican culture created a nation that in many ways was the opposite of its northern neighbor, with a flourishing tradition of art and poetry, yet with a stratified and unstable political economy.

SAN ANTONIO, A CITY AT THE CULTURAL CROSSROADS, 1719–1929

For a number of reasons, the city of San Antonio, Texas became a focal point of Mexican-American intellectual activity. From its inception, powerful forces tied it to the past and pulled it into the present. Founded in 1719 as a part of the global colonial competition between Spain and France, the city was an important military and religious center. A number of Catholic missions, including San Antonio de Valero (the Alamo) played an important part in the history of the entire region. Due to this connection to history, San Antonio, most especially its Tejano[30] population, has always been imbued with a deep sense of historical consciousness, what Richard Garcia referred to as "collective memory."[31] This memory, and the identity connected with it, were formed from San Antonio's early history as a Spanish colony and continued as the city took on a multicultural flavor and different groups, Tejano, southern Anglo-American, and Germans interacted. A student of the city in the mid 1960s believed that, "San Antonio has always charmed visitors with its cosmopolitan flavor and notably good natured [sic] atmosphere. Will Rogers, O. Henry and Sidney Lanier were enthusiasts of the city and, since they were among the leading critics of American life, San Antonians treasure their views."[32]

SAN ANTONIO UNDER SPAIN AND MEXICO, 1719–1836.

Perceiving a threat from its French rival, the Spanish monarchy created settlements in the province of Texas. These were in fact outposts of Mexican society, composed of soldiers that garrisoned the local fort, (or presidio), Franciscan missionaries attempting to convert native Americans to the Catholic faith and conform them to European culture, and immigrants from other parts of Mexico.

The Spanish-Mexican settlement of the frontier differed from Anglo-American expansion into the west. While U.S. settlement was driven largely by the private efforts of individuals and communities, Spanish expansion was initiated, carried out, and supervised by the Spanish viceroy. It was a reflection of the centralized semi-feudal mindset of the Spanish colonial system.

Such was the case in 1719, when a fort, a series of missions, and a small town arose on the banks of the San Antonio River. The city, known as San Antonio De Bexar, was augmented in 1731 by families from the Canary Islands. The original mestizo and Indian population, along with the new arrivals, created an atmosphere of racial diversity within a context of what

Timothy M. Matovina described as the "Mexican Catholic tradition."[33] That tradition was the result of the two hundred years of cultural contact between the Indian and Spanish cultures mentioned earlier.

The new city also became a picture of Mexican social hierarchy in miniature. Surveying the early history of San Antonio, Jesus de la Teja discovered that because of their European ancestry, the "immigrants from the Canary Islands held a special social status that they retained for two centuries."[34] In return for populating the frontier, the King of Spain granted noble title to former sheep and goat herders.[35]

The newcomers, known as Isleños, took control of the town government and demanded privileges regarding water rights and the dispersal of farm and ranch land. However, this class hierarchy was mitigated by the obstacles of desert, mountain, and sheer distance that conspired to create what Matovina believed was an independent Tejano identity.[36] San Antonio's physical isolation from central Mexico was only slightly less distant than the separation of the thirteen English Colonies from Great Britain, and the impact in creating a separate regional identity was almost the same. Second, as the centuries progressed, common difficulties, a shared culture and intermarriage "slowly fastened a joint identity on the town's population" according to de la Teja.[37] By 1800, a distinct character was formed among the people of San Antonio, which was unique to its environment, but was also distinctly Mexican.

AN EMERGING AMERICAN CITY, 1836–1920.

San Antonio underwent profound changes after Texas independence and statehood in 1845. The town went from a Mexican frontier outpost to a multicultural city on the southern edge of American expansion. This put new pressures on the Tejano population of San Antonio, and plunged them into a crisis of identity. Matovina observed, "The population of San Antonio was overwhelmingly Tejano until the U.S. annexation of Texas in 1845. By 1850, Tejanos numbered less than half of the local residents for the first time since the settlement's foundation, and the Anglo-American (*sic*) population began to rival them in size."[38] These new conditions forced Tejanos to choose between their identity as Texans and their cultural affiliation with Mexico.

ANGLOS

Most Anglo Americans who went to Texas came out of the hierarchical, slaveholding culture of the South that retained in many respects the feudal traditions of deference that vanished in the northern states, where individualism and small-scale capitalism held sway. Persons who visited Texas, however, found Anglo Texans to be the dregs of that system, the refugees from debt, dishonor, and economic depression.

Jose Maria Sanchez, a soldier in the Mexican army, formed an unfavorable opinion of the Anglos that were pouring into Texas after the Mexican independence. The new government allowed in Americans and Europeans, provided they observed Mexican laws. Very quickly, Mexicans like Sanchez had second thoughts about their decision when he encountered settlers such as Jared E. Groce, who was "a man of 45 to 50 years of age. He came from the United States to establish himself on the eastern bank of the Brazos River in order to avoid paying the numerous creditors that were suing him. He brought with him 116 slaves of both sexes, most of which were stolen. These wretched slaves are the ones who cultivate the corn and cotton, both of which yield copious crops to Mr. Groce. But he is a man who does not enjoy his wealth because he is extremely stingy, and he treats his slaves with great cruelty." Finally, in a grievous breach of the etiquette of hospitality, Sanchez and his other Mexican friends were forced to camp overnight outside of Groce's home.[39] From this and his visit to the settlement of San Filipe De Austin, Sanchez concluded "the Americans from the north are in general, in my opinion, lazy people of vicious character."[40]

Sanchez's experience represented the difficult relationship between the Tejano settlers and the Anglo American newcomers. Migration into Texas was part of an expansion of sixty years duration, rooted in the Scotch-Irish settlement of the Appalachian South. Arnoldo De Leon explained "[t]he great majority (of Anglo migrants) hailed from the Appalachians and South (sic) of the Ohio River . . . From this southern and frontier oriented culture they imported a certain suspicion of dark-skinned people and an obstinate belief that the mores of their own institutions should apply in the new color frontier."[41] While the image persists today of the South as a land of semi-feudal plantations where traditions of courtesy were prevalent, the actual picture was more complex. Most plantations (and many Tejano ranch and farmlands) were the extensions of a developing and growing capitalist system.[42] That system produced wealth for those involved; it also produced new social tensions. In the words of Everett Dick, "some of the newly rich had a tendency to form an arrogant aristocracy, with all the unlovely characteristics of the newly rich of any age."[43] Among those unlovely traits was a suspicion of strangers that Sanchez and later Fredrick Law Olmsted encountered.[44] In most cases, the manners and customs of white Southerners in Texas had more in common with the frontier than with the gentility of more settled regions.

Anglo movement into Texas was created in part by a rapidly growing population. Further, economic dislocation caused by the Panic of 1819 in the United States prompted the desire for more lands to the west. Stephen F. Austin from Virginia had arranged for settlements in Texas with the government of Mexico in 1821. To be admitted into Austin's colony, settlers had to agree to abide by the Mexican legal system, where slavery was forbidden and Roman Catholicism was the officially established church. Austin and his family agreed to abide by these conditions, but when Anglo

Americans achieved demographical superiority in the state, they reverted to their earlier patterns as slave-holders and Protestants.

Relations between Anglo Americans and Tejanos were complex and emotionally charged. Earlier settlers to the region frequented local society, conducted trade with both the United States and Mexico, and intermarried with Tejano families through the Texas Revolution in 1836 until the annexation of the area by the U.S. in 1845.[45] Thereafter, the Anglo community in the state applied a policy of expulsion of Mexicans that continued until the Civil War. Anglo minds justified the both legal and extralegal methods used in this effort by notions of racial superiority, Mexican atrocities during the Texan Revolution, and a sense of mission called Manifest Destiny. In reality, a greed for land on the part of speculators, squatters, and ranchers was the primary motivation.[46] Though the reaction of white Americans to Mexicans was like similar incidents in other parts of the Southwest, its southern character shaped how the Tejanos would respond to it, both in the short and long term. The actions of the Southerners are also critical in understanding the obstacles that Tejanos would face in gaining the civil rights due to them, and would set them apart from other ethnic groups.

Anglo Texans believed that the atrocities during the Revolution of 1836 at the Alamo and at the town of Goliad branded all Mexicans as a cruel and inhuman race, and that Tejanos were disloyal to the state and hostile to slavery. Regarding Texas historiography, David Montejano observed, "Although in many ways unnecessary for the task, Texan war memories facilitated the denigration of the Mexican." The Anglo interpretation of these events "constituted a ready-made and well developed body of myths, symbols, legends and explanations that were readily invoked to explain the peculiar society of Mexican Texas."[47] In fact, many Tejanos did help black slaves escape to Mexico, which only served to increase Anglo suspicion all the more. Southern Texans believed that "Mexicans stood as a constant threat, their associations and intercourse having dangerous and demoralizing consequences on an institution that stood as the very foundation of the southern American way."[48] When Anglos perceived that the source of their prosperity, namely their slaves, was threatened by Mexicans, they reacted vehemently against that risk. This was repeated when German Unionists faced the same attacks and threats upon their refusal to fight for the Confederacy.[49]

The dark skin and Indian ancestry also branded all Mexicans as inferior in the southern Anglo mind. De Leon believed that "Given the horror whites had developed concerning racial miscegenation during the two centuries of experience with blacks and Indians . . . the expressions of disdain toward the mixed-blood nature of Tejanos were very much congruent with the attitudes whites had always expressed."[50] Many have begun to argue that racism is grounded as much in economics and social class as in attitudes of cultural and racial difference. Montejano hypothesized that racism was largely a function of class when he quoted a South Texas educator in the 1920s: "The lower down the white man is the more he will object to the Mexicans. The lower class feels that the Mexican who is educated will try to be equal to him."[51] When defending slavery, many southerners began to argue that all cultures required what they called a "mudsill" class that kept all whites on the same level, regardless of character or economic achievement.[52] Sociologist Robert Blauner also acknowledged this in quoting from Confederate President Jefferson Davis: "(Black slavery) raises the white man to the same general level, that it dignifies and exalts every white man by the presence of a lower race."[53] The same pattern of racial thought that allowed southern whites to enslave Africans also permitted them to expel Tejanos from territory they desired. The unstable economics of the early nineteenth century Texas required the existence of mudsill races below which no white person would fall. It can therefore be argued that racism was a psychological device designed to protect the self-esteem of socially mobile and insecure Anglos in an economically volatile society, as was Texas in the nineteenth century.

What resulted was a pattern of violence, dispossession and extermination. So difficult had it become for Tejanos, even in San Antonio, that De Leon noted, "In 1858, two hundred families negotiated for their removal to Mexican soil because of injustices in Texas."[54] The plight of these citizens of Bexar could very well have been precipitated by the so-called "Cartman's War" of 1857. Envious of the business that Tejano teamsters had between the Texas Gulf coast and San Antonio, Anglo cartmen began a deliberate campaign of murder and violence. De Leon found that the bloodshed "attained such emotional heights that some feared a race war, others a genocidal venture against Mexicans."[55] According to Acuña, the number of dead Tejano cartmen reached an estimated figure of 75.[56] Eventually, the threat of economic repercussions and the awakening of dormant Anglo consciences forced authorities and newspapers to call for an end to the violence.[57]

The Cartman's War occurred within a background of increasing violence nationally, most of it regarding slavery. As southern whites perceived their "peculiar institution" threatened, many reacted by resorting to violence, which resulted in the Civil War.

Psychologically, Anglo Americans responded to a growing and unstable capitalist market with anxiety and insecurity. Southerners alleviated this anxiety by creating a racial caste system which placed them in a dominant position. In Texas during the nineteenth century, that caste system was directed against the earlier inhabitants of the state in the form of expulsion, and later segregation. For San Antonio, however, that segregation was never as complete as in other parts of Texas, or as it was against African Americans in the same time. One reason is that a legal body of "Jim Crow" laws was never enacted against Mexicans, although socially enforced boundaries existed. Matovina also reported limited social intermingling among the city's ethnic elites.[58] Nevertheless, Tejano San Antonio's class and kinship social system was replaced by one dominated by race and class. Southern Anglos assumed positions of economic and political power after Texas annexation, and profoundly altered the position and identity of Tejanos.

GERMANS

A German Texas ancestor of the famous Kleberg family related the romantic tale of "the rambunctious life and the bittersweet wedding of our wild son Sigismund, whose duel with the Prince of Prussia brought us all to Texas." After an Anglo Texan lost all of his estate to the German in a card game, "he looked around the room–his bride entered. He then drew the marriage certificate from his pocket, 'We'll play for that!' Instantly Sigismund pushed his winnings into the middle of the table. 'Certainly we will, but not without the consent of the lady.' She smiled, they played; Buckingham (the Anglo) lost. As Sigismund rose to consolidate the marriage certificate with his other winnings, Buckingham fired but missed, and as he reached for another pistol, Sigismund flashed his sword (the same that had killed the Prince of Prussia) and ran him through. The Coroner found self-defense. In a loud ringing voice the same official was heard to say, 'Will you, Barbara Buckingham, take this man?'"

How did the woman react to this violent episode?

"Dear sister: was ever woman in this manner wooed? Was ever woman in this manner won?'

'Hurry, hurry, and join us. Texas is truly the land of freedom and romance."[59]

For Germans coming to Texas in the mid-nineteenth century, the new land was truly different from the very conservative, traditional life they had known. After a letter by a German immigrant was published in 1831, a private association headed by nobles and budding capitalists organized an association for the purpose of colonizing the state eleven years later.[60] Most of the immigrants were German liberals fleeing the politically and socially conservative Germany. Glen Lich noted, "Many of the German colonists were well educated. In this respect (they) were following a pattern much like the Puritans of New England . . . who recognized that knowledge was the conveyor of civilization."[61] Most of the Germans moved into designed ethnic communities north of San Antonio that were enclaves of their culture, such as New Braunfels and Fredericksburg. But many, rejecting the organic discipline of these settlements, moved into cities like San Antonio.

What was the relationship between the Germans and the Tejano community? The famous northern city planner, Frederick Law Olmsted, when traveling to view conditions in the South, looked into the history of San Antonio's multi-ethnic community that so differed from other cities he had visited. According to him, in 1854 there was a lynching and a plot by the sheriff to create a posse in order to drive the Mexican community from the town they founded and built. The plan was thwarted, however, by the Germans, who "were of the opinion . . . that this was not the right and republican way." Olmsted also discovered, "One of them, who lived on the Medina (River), told us he had no complaint to make of the Mexicans; they never stole his property nor troubled him in any way."[62] While knowledge of relations between the German and Tejano communities in San Antonio is not extensive, it seems that during the pre-Civil war era, the two groups coexisted rather peacefully. The egalitarian attitude of Germans toward Mexicans and their hostility toward slavery led to friction between southern Anglos and the immigrants, and outright violence during the Civil War. After the war and into the twentieth century, the desire of German Texans to assimilate led them, for the most part, to adopt the racial proclivities of the surrounding white population.

TEJANOS

The tragic situation of Juan Seguín, a founder of the Texas republic, was typical of the crisis of identity brought about by the changing ethnic situation in San Antonio. Seguín was a leader in the Texas Revolutionary army and mayor of San Antonio during the Texas Republic. As such, he and much of the community had cast their lot politically with Texas. Concerning the Tejano dilemma, Matovina wrote, "They were native Texans who had consistently promoted regional interests in their dealings with state and local officials. But they were also Mexican Catholics who valued their cultural and religious heritage."[63] Seguín was the personification of a group that was about to be caught between two cultures, Mexican and American.

In 1842, during an invasion of San Antonio by the Mexican army, the army's commander, Rafael Vásquez, invited the Tejano population to return to Mexico, "and announced that . . . Seguín was still a loyal Mexican." David Weber concluded, "Vásquez appears to have been deliberately trying to discredit Seguín, and the plan succeeded, for Seguín had Anglo enemies who were eager to believe anything that would remove him from power."[64] These adversaries used Vásquez's assertion as a pretext to remove the mayor from office, drive him from San Antonio and take his property. In time the melancholy Seguín had to take refuge in Mexico, serving in its army to avoid being jailed for treason. He described himself in his memoir "a victim to the wickedness of a few men [and] *a foreigner in my native land;* [my emphasis] could I be expected stoically to endure their outrages and insults? Crushed by sorrow, convinced that my death alone would satisfy my enemies, I sought for a shelter amongst those . . . whom I fought. I separated from my country, parents, family, relatives and friends, and what was more, from the institutions on behalf of which I had drawn my sword, with an earnest wish to see Texas free and happy."[65]

Seguín's memoir, as a record of one victimized by Manifest Destiny's assumptions of Anglo racial superiority, is comparable with the autobiography of Frederick Douglass, who as a black slave was subject to the other racial injustice of America. As Douglass did, Seguín appealed to the sense of justice professed in the American system.[66] Seguín also had to refute false racial stereotypes, in his case, that all Mexicans were to be suspected of disloyalty to Texas and the United States. In the end, unfortunately, Seguín was forced to leave San Antonio, a fate typical of many elite Tejanos during and after the Mexican War. Weber discovered the assertion of San Antonio's Catholic "Bishop Odin [that] twenty prominent Texano [*sic*] families left San Antonio in 1842 and countless others joined them."[67] Montejano also perceived the change that came over the city, when by 1856, the population was almost evenly divided between Anglos, Tejanos, and Germans. In his view, "The San Antonio of Olmsted was quite different from the San Antonio of Juan Seguín only twelve years before."[68]

Tejanos found themselves caught in the middle between their Mexican-Catholic heritage and their loyalty to their region.[69] As Anglo American encroachment grew, the conflict in loyalties also grew. Many Tejanos responded by returning, at least temporarily, across the Rio Grande. But for the ones who stayed, the Mexican and Texas traditions continued being determinants in their lives and identities. One San Antonio Tejano gave the following answer: "When asked in later years if he loved Texas more than Mexico . . . Enrique Esparza reportedly stated that he was of mixed Indian and Spanish blood and was proud of that ancestry. He then added that he saw his father die for Texas in the battle of the Alamo and that he was proud to be a Texan and an American."[70]

TEJANO EARLY TRADITIONS, 1846–1920

From its inception until Reconstruction, San Antonio's economy depended on agriculture from the surrounding area; as a frontier outpost of Spain, Mexico and the United States, it was removed from the national market evolving elsewhere. The end of the Civil War, however, brought two innovations: the arrival of commercial ranching and the railroad, which both economically connected San Antonio to the rest of the nation and brought immigration from the rest of the United States.[71] The changeover from an early local capitalist agricultural economy to a national one also resulted in the political power moving from Mexican (Tejano) hands into those of Anglo-Americans (mainly former Southerners and German immigrants). This segregation, however, had an important byproduct. In contrasting the relationship between Anglos and Mexican Americans in Texas and California, Acuña notes that "In Texas, Chicanos suffered more from segregation and racial barriers. Texas was a southern state with all the social, political, and intellectual limitations of the South. This isolation encouraged a cohesiveness among Tejanos. Therefore, it is not surprising that LULAC (League of United Latin American Citizens), which had chapters in California and throughout the Southwest, was in the last analysis a Texas affair."[72] Because, or in spite of the fact that Tejanos found themselves politically and economically disenfranchised within the larger Texas society, within their own communities they were still able to maintain a strong sense of Mexican-Catholic identity.

POETRY AND THE BORDER HERO.

After Texas was admitted as a state in 1845, Tejanos socially, politically, and economically were overwhelmed by the migration of Anglo-American settlers, making the original inhabitants strangers in a land that had once been theirs. A Chicano cited the work of an earlier Texas historian in asserting, "on the Border after 1848 the Mexican was 'victimized by the law,' that 'the old landholding families found their titles in jeopardy and if they did not lose in the courts they lost to their American lawyers' and again that 'the Mexicans suffered not only in their persons but in their property.'"[73] Whether they were overwhelmed by Gold Rush squatters in California or intimidated by Texas Rangers, Mexican Americans found themselves reduced to second-class status.

"By the rivers of Babylon, we sat down and wept, when we remembered Zion."[74] As it was with the ancient Israelites in the Babylonian captivity or the individual condition of women such as Emily Dickinson, poetry often was the language of the dispossessed and the outsider. With a tradition of expressive poetry and music already within their culture, Mexican Americans in the Southwest used verse both to describe their physical and emotional condition and to serve as a vehicle of vicarious resistance to Anglo discrimination.

This was particularly true in the case of Gregorio Cortez, a Tejano who was a fugitive from the law in 1901. His escape from the unjust pursuit of the Texas Rangers and local police made him a legend among his people and the subject of heroic ballads, or *corridos*. Américo Paredes observed that Cortez became the personification of the virtuous Mexican American persecuted by the Anglo. One version of the corrido sings,

> Then said Gregorio Cortez
> With his pistol in his hand,
> 'Ah, how many cowardly rangers
> Against one lone Mexican!'[75]

Every Mexican found in Cortez something to identify with. In Paredes' estimation, Cortez "became in the legend a synthesis of the Border Mexican" who vicariously applied to the fugitive "his own disagreeable contacts with the Anglo-American."[76] Along with other similar heroes who fell outside the laws of the Anglo southwest, Cortez became an archetype of Mexican resistance.

As the story of Cortez was embellished, he was given superb qualities of character, courage, cunning, and industry. These tales transformed him into a figure of folklore comparable to Anglo-American tales of Davy Crockett and Mike Fink, who were the personification of Anglo-American frontier virtues. Cortez's betrayal by another Mexican just before an escape across the Rio Grande repeated a tragic motif in Mexican literature and history dating back to the fall of the Aztec Empire. Many times Mexico and Mexicans seemed to be betrayed either by one of their own or by a fatal flaw in character that led to their downfall, a theme as old as the ancient Greeks.

Early Mexican Americans perceived themselves to be outsiders on the American scene. For reasons of politics, economics, language, geography, and race, most Tejanos were tied to their former homeland rather than the United States. By both their choice and that of the Anglo-American community, they remained culturally and physically distinct. Because of this, their values and perspectives remained one with the largely pre-capitalist environment of Mexico.

Paredes also believed that the legend and ballads created in Cortez's honor were the product of a pre-Enlightenment culture that was geographically isolated and which passed down its traditions in non-literate forms. He asserted that "The Lower Rio Grande people lived in conditions in which folk cultures develop. They lived in isolation from the main currents of world events. They preferred to live in small, isolated communities that were interested in their own problems. Their type of social organization was the family holding or the communal village, ruled by patriarchal authority under a kind of pre-eighteenth century democracy."[77] This description would also be accurate for nearly all Mexican-American communities prior to 1913. Conditions either of geography, demographics, or racial prejudice put the Tejano into insular groups apart from the rest of United States culture. Mexicans of all regions saw themselves as a persecuted outsider group, but one which demanded respect.

Chapter Two

Visions of Community, Part I

THE IMMIGRANT VOICE: *LA PRENSA*

In his synthesis of intellectual and social history, Thomas Bender discovered that "different cultures of intellectual life may succeed each other; they may also vie for hegemony within a given society."[1] David A. Hollinger also discussed the community context in the life of the mind when he asserted that "discourse and the communities formed around it are 'central subjects' as authentic as are ideas and the texts in which ideas are embedded."[2] Between 1913 and 1945, communities of discourse competed for the hearts and minds of San Antonio's Mexican-American population, offering different visions of identity.

The first group was comprised of an elite class of Mexican professionals and intellectuals who were forced out of their native land by the violence of the Mexican Revolution. They saw San Antonio as a place of refuge where they could carry out their political and literary agenda until the *ancien regime* was restored (in the same way as Cuban exiles in South Florida after the Cuban Revolution of 1958). The intellectual focus of the exile elite was therefore in Mexico, not in the United States. The exiles sought to maintain their identity and culture as Mexicans. In the words of Mario Garcia, "they possessed a Mexican dream, not an American dream."[3]

An American-born middle class that made its living in professional occupations formed the second group. Angered and embarrassed by segregation, discrimination, and acts of racial prejudice by the Anglo Texan community, this emerging cohort resolved to confront this burden through organized action. Their emphasis was on the lives they lived in the United States. As a group on the make whose roots often reached to San Antonio's founding, the Tejano middle class desired to stake their claim to equal status as Texans and Americans. Their participation in the World Wars made their assertions more justifiable and their methods more assertive and militant, as Mario Garcia discovered. "Coming of political age during the reform period of the New Deal and experiencing the patriotic idealism generated by World War II, Mexican Americans expected more from American life than immigrants." A new outlook was created by these circumstances; "For Mexican Americans there was no going back to Mexico. The United States was their home. They hungrily pursued the American dream."[4]

In 1929, middle class Mexican Americans formed the League of United Latin American Citizens (LULAC) to promote civil rights for Mexican Americans and to educate the Tejano community of their status as citizens. Alonso Perales, one of LULAC's architects, wrote "My only purpose in forming said organization is to bring about the rapid intellectual, social, and political evolution of Americans of Mexican descent and to produce the highest type of Mexican possible."[5]

Perales and the rest of the middle class enlisted the principles of liberalism and individualism that were the ideological foundation of Anglo-American society. LULAC used both the rhetoric of classical liberalism and the methods of twentieth century progressivism to attain legal and social quality for Tejanos. Because many of LULAC's leadership were attorneys, they had a natural affinity for due process, a belief that individuals should be ruled by their consent, and that society could be changed by educated persons. They also endorsed the political ideals of the Enlightenment articulated by Thomas Jefferson and Thomas Paine regarding the equality of all people.

San Antonio became the scene of competition between LULAC on the one hand and the Mexican immigrant elite that created *La Prensa* on the other. The former wanted to create an American identity for Tejanos within a liberal political consensus; the latter decided to keep a collective political and national identity that was Mexican and conservative.

Yet, in important ways, the exile elite and the San Antonio middle class were alike. Both groups (though for different reasons) had an abiding faith in human progress. Maintaining pride in Mexican cultural traditions and community was crucial for both. Finally, their minority status within their society and the personal quality of Mexican politics tended to create elitism among the upper and middle classes of this community.

What distinguished each was their vision for themselves and their vast audience of impoverished Mexican immigrants. Would that future be Mexican or American? As Richard Garcia said, "LULAC faced north and pursued the reality of everyday existence in the United States, [and] looked toward the present and the future. The *Ricos* (the elite) however, always faced south and remembered the past and wished to continue it. Regardless of their exile in the United States, they continued to be Mexicans from Mexico."[6] Even the Mexico they wished to return to had changed drastically during the Mexican Revolution. The aspiration of the elite was to return, both in time and space.

The voice that gave rise to *La Prensa* was part of a recent tradition of Mexican revolutionary activity in San Antonio. In 1904 radical opponents of the regime of Mexican President Porfirio Diaz resided in the city and attempted to gain local support. Ricardo and Enrique Flores-Magón, the group's leaders, formed the Club Líberal de San Antonio and the anarchist newspaper *Regeneración*. According to Marta Cotera, the Club Líberal was distinctive because of the direct participation of women, marking the earliest beginnings of a Mexican-American feminism.[7] The budding radical movement ended when threats of prosecution by the U.S. and Mexican governments forced the Magóns to leave Texas and settle eventually in California.

In 1910, the exiled Francisco Madero became the second revolutionary in San Antonio fleeing Mexican authorities. Desiring to return to Mexico and institute a liberal democratic government, Madero and his followers formed a community in exile with personal and business ties to San Antonio. From there, Madero also published his *Plan De San Luis Potosí*, his reform program for Mexico. Unlike the Flores Magóns, Madero had an extensive network of social and political support in the city.[8] Although he successfully gained the Mexican presidency in 1911, Madero's new government collapsed when he was assassinated two years later. Years of bloody revolution were triggered that would engulf Mexicans on both sides of the Rio Grande and cause hundreds of thousands to flee into the United States. These new immigrants would be a part of the second stage of San Antonio's Mexican community. In fact, "[the] dominant theme of Chicano history (sic) in the twentieth century is immigration" in the opinion of historian Manuel Gonzales.[9]

Because of this change, many Mexicans, including Ignacio Lozano (1886–1953), were forced to leave and seek asylum in the United States. In 1913 (when the revolution had taken a critical turn) Lozano began publishing a Spanish-language daily, *La Prensa*, in his adopted home of San Antonio. Featuring journalistic descriptions and editorials on the events in Mexico and World War I, *La Prensa* was an important intellectual vehicle of expatriates living in the United States. According to Manuel Ruiz Ibañez, "among the editorial staff and writers of *La Prensa* there were lawyers, engineers, educators and philosophers who had chosen San Antonio as an asylum, but all of them were outstanding writers." This was confirmed by "Philosopher Jose Vasoncelos, who once said 'I doubt that any paper in Latin America has ever been able to gather such illustrious pens as *La Prensa*.'"[10]

Lozano and others were the leaders of Mexican society during the presidency of Porfirio Diaz, a dictator who determined to bring modern industrial and technological progress to Mexico. This progress produced the side effects of greater foreign (U.S. and European) control of the Mexican economy, the continued repression of liberal reform politics, and the aggravation of social stratification that was the norm in Mexico since the colonial period. The end of Diaz' presidency in 1910 ignited a social and political revolution that drove large numbers of elite Mexicans into the

United States. This exiled class set themselves apart from the English speaking U.S., from the radical political developments in their homeland, and even from the pre-existing Mexican-American community. Along these lines, Ruben Mungia (son of an early employee of the paper and the uncle of San Antonio mayor Henry Cisneros) declared, "The people who came here and hoped for a quick restoration of the Diaz regime or a similar conservative government . . . remained aloof both of their Anglo hosts who also had only recently arrived in this area as well as of their brown cousins who could trace their beginnings here for ages prior to the Conquistadores of Mother Spain." In response, "These people built here a colony, a colony of Mexicans. They had their stores, their schools, their churches, their clubs, their professionals and they had their newspaper—*La Prensa*."[11]

Local happenings normally took up barely half a page of the paper's content. The global emphasis was consistent with Lozano's vision for the paper, which was to serve as a free platform from which its writers could inform their readers of important international events much in the same way that political expatriates from Ireland, Cuba and countless other nations have done. Next to nothing was said about their experience in Texas. From this we can gather that Lozano and his fellow writers saw themselves as temporary sojourners in the United States, biding time until they could return to Mexico and resume their place in its elite. In the first issue, the editors wrote "we will always publish the most interesting news, as much of Europe as of America, principally Mexico."[12]

Over the decades, *La Prensa* became a catalyst for the Mexican Americans because it created a community of discourse that united both the wealthy intellectuals and their impoverished countrymen who accompanied them. This community of discourse resulted in the political awareness, which in turn laid the groundwork for the political and social activism of the 1930s and 40s. As Mungia noted, "*La Prensa*, a conservative paper, can well lay claim to having awakened the liberal thinking of men such as M.C. Gonzalez, Mauro Machado . . . Santiago Tafolla . . . and thousands of Garcias, Lopez, Martinez, etc. who no longer sought to return to the old country and who finally realized they belonged and organized vibrant, aggressive organizations such as the Knights of America, Sons of America and LULAC to insure for the new citizen, the Mexican American, his right to life, liberty and the pursuit of happiness."[13]

This unforeseen effect of *La Prensa* as a unifying force in the community proved to be its undoing. When Mexican Americans changed the focus of their activism toward the United States, the paper (written in Spanish with a primarily Mexican focus) ceased to be relevant and was closed in 1958. However, *La Prensa* marked an important transition from the first generation of Mexican immigrants to their children, whose intellectual attention was now focused on seeking identity as Americans. Later generations of Tejanos, the "children of *La Prensa*" wanted to become full participants on the American scene. As they pursued this, their understanding of the United States, and of themselves, changed as well.

LULAC: ENTERING THE LIBERAL MAINSTREAM

The 1949 convention of the League of United Latin-American Citizens (LULAC) was held in San Antonio, Texas. That convention's many activities included a quiz program, moderated by former LULAC president M.C. Gonzales. Among the several questions he asked his panel of "experts" were "What does it mean to be born a Latin American Citizen in Texas?" Awkward silence came from his panel and the audience. Finally, "a very young man stood up, and in his clear but youthful voice gave the definition: 'To be born a Latin American in Texas is to be given an opportunity to make a great and unique contribution to our State and Nation."[14]

This young man was the spokesperson for an entire generation of middle class Mexican Americans who desired full integration into the American mainstream. Like Benjamin Franklin during the Revolutionary era and Booker T. Washington at the turn of the century, the Mexican Americans of the mid-twentieth century wanted to prove their worthiness to be included into the economic, political, and social system. They did not question the ultimate justice of that system; these sons of immigrants wanted a chance to be included in it. The rise of a Mexican-American middle class during the post World War I era made possible the beginnings of organized intellectual activity among their leadership, just as a similar development occurred in colonial America and among turn-of-the-20th-century African Americans.

LULAC and its forebears came into being in response to unbridled racial hatred that held Mexican Americans to the lowest rung of Texas society, to the point that their very lives were considered of little value. Jose Amaro Hernandez stated bluntly that in the early twentieth century, "the killing of a Chicano by an Anglo was not considered a crime in Texas," and "[l]ynching of Chicanos became almost commonplace."[15] During the post-World War II era, Stuart Barnes observed that attitudes, for the most part, had not improved. "Talk to the average Texan. Texans do not like the 'Mexes.' They will tell you so. Some will try to justify their hatred and discrimination. The majority do not bother. For the most part, it is an intent, blind unreasoned prejudice that admits of no questioning, no argument."[16]

In 1915 the inter-racial tensions flared into open violence when Tejanos in deep South Texas attempted to end their economic and political disenfranchisement. The *Plan De San Diego* proposed to create an army of Mexicans, blacks, and Japanese immigrants that would expel or kill all whites in the Southwest and declare an independent republic based in San Antonio. Raids by Tejanos that destroyed Anglo lives and property were met with overwhelming reprisals by white Texans including the dreaded Texas Rangers. The slaughter was such that local newspapers treated the murders as commonplace.[17] With the showing of the motion picture *The Birth of a Nation* that same year, violence against Mexicans took place within a national context of racial fear and hatred. Montejano believed "there was general agreement, in Texas and elsewhere, that Mexicans were not legitimate citizenry of the United States. They were outside the civic order, and references to American national integrity and Texas history were often ill-disguised claims of Anglo supremacy."[18] Prejudice by the dominant community exacerbated class tensions within Mexican-American society, angering the middle class. It also caused them, in Richard Garcia's words "to separate themselves from the Mexican laboring class and the Mexican migrants."[19] The increase of Mexican immigration after 1913 also worsened Anglo prejudice, causing a disparaging of Mexican identity. "As one sociologist related, [the Mexican identity was] associated with illiteracy, shiftlessness, and a myriad of other uncomplimentary characteristics."[20] In the face of such discrimination, Tejano identity was extremely problematic. In her history of the Mexican-American civil rights movement, Cynthia Orozco related that "in 1918, the headline of *Democrata Fronterizo*, a Laredo [Texas] newspaper, read 'The children of Mexican citizens who are born in the United States are Americans' as if a new discovery had been made. Despite the Treaty of Guadalupe Hidalgo, many Tejanos were unaware of their U.S. citizenship."[21]

To combat both violence and racial prejudice, Tejanos developed organizations of mutual assistance, or *mutualistas*. Mutual assistance organizations were common among Mexican Americans since the nineteenth century. Their purpose was fraternal, civic, and protective. Mutualistas were pivotal in that they were often the first organized attempts by Tejanos to deal with discrimination. At the same time, their focus on communal assistance and the use of the Mexican consulate as an avenue for redress of grievances revealed that many members of mutualistas still saw themselves as Mexicans, rather than Americans. However, in their voluntaristic emphasis and organizational autonomy, mutualistas were a part of an increasing acculturation to American thinking.[22] Increasingly they began to work within the American legal system for protection (through a rising generation of Tejano attorneys, such as Perales). La Gran Liga Mexicana (The Grand Mexican League) a San Antonio mutualista, was an example of this trend. Hernandez discovered that, "La Gran Liga was preoccupied with protecting the civil rights of Chicanos in American courts."[23]

Because they often allowed women as full members, mutualistas were important instruments of political socialization for them. In her dissertation, "Lenninger Pycior identified nineteen mutualistas in San Antonio, seven of which permitted women to hold office."[24] What voice women would have within Tejano advocacy groups or what input they would have in shaping their identity became an important (and at times divisive) issue.

Mutualistas provided an outlet for Tejano grievances and were the first collective attempt at defense and community action. They served some of the same functions for Mexican Americans that black evangelical churches did for the African American community.[25] Mutualistas became the basis for developing a middle class leadership and a new social identity to persons victimized by racial hatred. As Hernandez concluded, "the basic idea in the movement for [unifying mutualistas] was a desire for defense and filling acute needs."[26]

In the 1920s, unity was the one objective that eluded Tejano organizations. At an informal meeting in San Antonio in 1921 that attempted to create a single civil rights organization, participants literally came to blows over who would lead the proposed group.[27] In spite of this early rancor, the pressing need for such an association to defend the rights of Mexicans forced the middle class to make several important decisions that would impact their identity for several decades. The exclusion of Mexican citizens and the use of English as their official language positioned middle class activists as Americans wanting full access to the American dream.

Two events provided the impetus for the coalescence of a Mexican-American mindset. The first was the terrible discrimination and race prejudice. The second was the presence of Mexican Americans in World War I.[28] Returning Tejano veterans were not nearly as tolerant of racial prejudice as before, due in large part to the merit-based environment of the military. Professor J. Luz Saenz, a veteran of the war, bitterly recalled, "We were accepted, but during our entire military life, we felt a humiliating load of distrust on our shoulders . . . We knew under what conditions we were fighting. It was under 100% prejudice." He also added, "After demobilization in World War I it took only three days after we received our Honorable Discharge [sic] to throw us out from restaurants and deny us service as human beings."[29]

Veterans like Saenz and Alonso Perales believed their military service earned them an equal position to Anglos in civilian life. Instead, like African Americans in the South, they found the stigma of racial inferiority pressed upon them with even greater force. After the war, middle class Tejanos began to form organizations that would correct this injustice and improve their position in San Antonio's society.

In 1921 the Order Sons of America (OSA) was founded in an attempt to meet the need for a communal response to discrimination. Begun by attorney Santiago Tafolla, Sr., the OSA was patterned after the mutualistas.[30] Along with Tafolla were prominent San Antonians Don Pedro Hernandez and his wife Maria Latigo Hernandez, whose writing and activism would span over half a century. The involvement of women and the use of Spanish were important contributions of mutualistas. However, the focus of the OSA on improving conditions for Tejanos within the local community was a step toward the creation of a Mexican-American agenda.

Although the OSA formed a number of chapters in South Texas and engineered several victories for Tejano opportunity, it was weakened by numerous internal rivalries and issues. From its beginning, the group was impaired by personal animosities, an unfortunate trait that would plague Mexican-American activism until the present. This was compounded by the conflict between Tafolla and other Tejano leaders over the leadership style of the OSA. Influenced by the very personal style of leadership that typified both Mexican and San Antonian political history, Tafolla wanted absolute control of any civil rights group. Other activists such as Perales, Ben Garza of Corpus Christi, and M.C. Gonzales of San Antonio, wanted an entity that was organizational in its polity, rather than personal. They desired a system based on the American constitutional paradigm. It can therefore be argued that Tafolla wanted to create a body that was Mexican (personalistic) in its operation, while others fought for a body that worked on a liberal, American model.[31]

This conflict exposed the basic dilemma that Mexican Americans faced in their interaction with United States culture: how far could they go in assuming American intellectual habits, either politically or socially, and still retain their own culture, their own sense of "Mexicanness?" This difficulty was illustrated by George J. Sanchez when he related the problem of a Mexican in Los Angeles who needed to obtain American citizenship in order to defend the rights of his community, an option he found to be personally repugnant.[32] No other immigrant group has had to face this problem. For European and Asian immigrants coming to the United States, there was an existential "break" involved in crossing a wide ocean to a new nation. Mexicans did not have this same sense of departing in time and space. For them the issues of citizenship and identity were far more problematic and were confronted by successive groups of Mexican immigrants.[33]

Middle class Tejanos grappled with the issue of identity as they attempted to unite against discrimination. Throughout their history, they were forced to deal with both external pressures (Anglo racism) and less obvious internal problems of identity. On August 14, 1927, this came to the forefront when leaders from the OSA and other bodies gathered in Harlingen, Texas to hammer out a state-wide civil rights organization. The meeting foundered when delegates who were Mexican citizens were excluded from membership. In response, they walked out of the convention.

Tejanos like Perales felt that citizenship created different agendas for Mexicans and Tejanos. Orozco later concurred when she wrote that the "goal of the Mexican-American [sic] was 'Americanization,' and the aim of Mexicans was the cultivation of Mexican nationalism (as expressed by the exiles through *La Prensa*)."[34]

A crucial turning point in the formulation of a Mexican-American identity was reached at the Harlingen convention. There the middle class consciously separated its ideological destiny from that of Mexico and linked itself with the United States. Though little was resolved politically in Harlingen, a fraternity that was American in its organizational polity, national identity, and language was first conceived.

This meeting called for the eventual unification of all regional Tejano organizations under a single umbrella. When Tafolla's OSA chapter balked at the merger for personal reasons, Perales, M.C. Gonzales, and Ben Garza convened a gathering on February 18, 1929 in the coastal city of Corpus Christi. The League of United Latin American Citizens was created on that date.[35]

The explicit goal of LULAC's founders was the formation of a Mexican-American self-consciousness that would uplift the entire ethnic community and, most importantly, be respected by Texas Anglos. LULAC member Adolf Garza defined the problem faced by Tejanos as follows: "They are neither Mexicans in fact nor Americans in heart. If they go to Mexico they are called Texano [sic], if they are among the Americans of English or Saxon origin, they not Americans but 'Mescans.' And where does that place us? No where, we are men without a country."[36]

LULAC believed that dissonance could be removed through a combination of self-help, civic education, and direct (non-violent) action in mainstream society designed to end discrimination in the school system and other public places. Reminiscent of W. E. B. Dubois, LULAC self-consciously served as the intellectual vanguard that would bring about a change of mind and attitude among Tejanos. In 1931, Adolf Garza admonished, "The truth of the matter is that we are not man enough, brave enough nor intelligent enough to tell the world that we are not 'Mescans' that we are Texans and proud of it. We must be courageous enough to demand our place."[37]

The constitution of LULAC drawn up in May of 1929 reflected the liberal, American emphasis of the middle class. Its overall purpose was "to develop within members of our race the best, purest, and most perfect type of true and loyal citizen of the United States of America." LULAC hoped to achieve this aim through objectives outlined in the remainder of the constitution. 1) English would be the official language of the organization. 2) All members were expected to reverence and obey the laws and Constitution of the U.S. 3) Rights, protection of the laws and opportunity should be given equally to all, and all legal means will be used to bring this about. 4) The education of children in the language and customs of the U.S. was encouraged. 5) Although LULAC itself was non-partisan, it would promote the active participation of its members and the Tejano community in the political process and would support only those officeholders that advocated the interests of that community. 6) Finally, they pledged to set up funds for both mutual protection and education.[38]

The belief that institutions and individuals could be reformed through education and organized, reasonable change was an expression of the liberal direction that they were taking the Tejano community. Richard Garcia observed, "This rising middle class sought to maintain a Mexican consciousness of collectivity even though it was accepting Lockian [sic] idealism and Jeffersonian emphasis of individualism and the reality of James Madison's and the New Deal's emphasis on political pluralism."[39]

The statements and actions of LULAC's founders expressed a strong belief in the natural rights tradition that was a part of America's original legal system. Their Catholic-Mexican heritage and family structure gave them an intuitive deference for authority; their education in the United States directed that deference to the personalities and ideals of Jefferson, Madison, and Lincoln. Richard Garcia noted this trend. "Even as the Mexican American middle class was convinced of the American political system through Texas schools, they felt that equal access to education would uplift the rest of the community."[40]

Lastly, liberal trends were evidenced by the emphasis of LULAC on local councils, or chapters, and the limited power of the national leadership reflected a desire for individual and local autonomy. This was both a weakness and a strength for the organization. While emphasizing a local structure encouraged the growth of grass-roots leadership, it inhibited the formation of a national organization with a unifying ideology and agenda. This tendency also reflected the difficulty for Mexican Americans in forming a united front against Anglo authority structures.

As Garcia detailed, "The ideas expressed in the [LULAC] constitution were not the ideas of just an organization; they formed the ideology of an emerging middle class mentality." It is not an exaggeration to argue that in February 1929, the organizers of LULAC believed that they were replicating the events of 1776. By embracing the language, politics and ideology of Jeffersonian America, they were laying claim to its promises for persons of Mexican descent. In this sense, the Corpus Christi convention and the document it produced were comparable to the Second Continental Congress and its product, the Declaration of Independence.[41]

In addition to the classical liberalism of the Revolutionary period, members of LULAC were listening to contemporary currents of progressive thought. Anglo American progressive writers and activists (such as Herbert Croly and Jane Addams) were urging a more active role for government in addressing the problems of contemporary America, among them the cultural questions posed by the growing immigrant population. Although Progressivism would have a negative impact for Chicano identity in California, Orozco found that Tejanos endorsed "a new way of thinking that revolved around organization. New words such as professional, expert, and system became commonplace. This ideology primarily affected the college-educated Tejanos and [can] especially be seen in the writing of several lawyers, especially Alonso S. Perales [who] would advance this ideology and it was reflected in the LULAC constitution."[42]

Historians influenced by the Chicano cultural movement of the nineteen sixties have accused LULAC and its supporters of abandoning their Mexican cultural identity and of representing only a small number of Tejanos. Montejano asserted that, "The civil rights campaigns of the small Texas Mexican middle class suggest what the emergence of this class signified for the culture of racism . . . they pressed for the rights of respectable educated

Mexicans."[43] Acuña's *Occupied America*, long considered an important work on Chicano history, argued that LULAC "[d]id not really serve the interests of the poor, but rather [sic] reflected the philosophy of the middle class, who wanted assimilation."[44]

The heterogeneous nature of Tejano society and the totally disenfranchised position of its community in San Antonio are not taken into account in these criticisms. Since the majority of Mexican Americans were barred from voting, serving on juries, or receiving a quality education, the middle class was the only group that had the ability to speak on behalf of those who could not. One instance during the thirties bears this out. Malcolm Ross attended a San Antonio dinner at which prominent middle and upper class Tejanos feted four workers who were recently promoted to supervisor. Ross poignantly observed of the LULAC group: "Their group interest was strong because their personal interests were deeply involved. Their tidy bank balances, their pleasant homes, and their confidence in their own abilities could not make them fully citizens so long as the great mass of their people were set apart and kept in squalor."[45] Emotion, family and culture tied LULAC to the majority of poor Mexicans and Tejanos, as it was for black Americans such as Booker T. Washington and W. E. B. Dubois.

LULAC also had critics in its own time. Pedro and Maria Hernandez argued that the split between the OSA and the new organization were as much over identity issues like language and the equal inclusion of women as it was over the leadership style of Tafolla.[46] With the dissolution of the OSA, the Hernandezes founded their own civil rights group, Los Orden Caballeros de America (Order Knights of America) in 1929. They continued to have an active role in politics and civil advocacy on both sides of the border for several decades.

To conceive of LULAC as accommodationist or opportunist would be a mistake. The early professionals who were its constituency attempted to plot an unknown course through a hostile sea of racial prejudice. Guadalupe San Miguel concluded that "[t]his group of individuals was not calling for the total assimilation of the Mexican-American population into Anglo cultural society as has been suggested by some authors. Integration into Anglo American political and social life was to be a selective process."[47] For LULAC's founders, Mexican-American identity was comprised of a culturally Mexican and politically American ethos. In Richard Garcia's words, LULAC would incorporate "[b]oth the U.S. and Mexican conditions of thought—Americans within a consensus of liberal thought [the rights of the individual], but Mexican within a consensus of culture."[48]

This consensus allowed LULAC to assume ideological leadership of the Tejano community as the Victorian middle class had done for New York City Americans in the nineteenth century.[49] Through *La Prensa* and the English-language newspapers of San Antonio, LULAC was able to deliver its message. For them, (as it was for Booker T. Washington and Dubois) that message was that the only path to social and political equality was the path of education. It was that drive that led them into political activity on the state, local and national level.

ALONSO S. PERALES

Two San Antonio attorneys were the intellectuals whose activities gave rise to the LULAC mindset. Alonso Perales (1898–1960) and Manuel C. Gonzales (1900–1986) self-consciously sought to create a pluralistic identity among the Tejano population, linking pride in Mexican cultural identity with participation in the American political and economic system. Their thinking "was the central ideology of LULAC in particular and the Mexican American mind in general." According to Richard Garcia, "for both, being in LULAC, fighting for the poorer Mexican community, fighting against discrimination, changing Mexicans into U.S. citizens, and developing a love for the United States was being a Mexican American."[50] Although the two men agreed with the ideology of LULAC, they disagreed as to the means and the ends of Tejano empowerment and reflected the tension in the LULAC consensus. Gonzales uncritically embraced American individualism in both its political and cultural implications. On the other hand, Perales desired to retain the communal distinctiveness of Mexican culture in a more ethnically tolerant society. The writings and actions of both reflected the conflict between a decentralized individualism and a centralized nation that valued family, history, and tradition, as did Hamilton and Jefferson in the early days of the American republic. Richard Garcia believed, "Perales sought a democratic America with separate ethnic groupings; Gonzales saw a socially integrated America, but with individual cultural rights."[51]

Alonso S. Perales spent a lifetime fighting against the barriers of prejudice raised against himself and the members of his race. Orphaned at age six, he was a product of the public schools of Alice, Texas and a business college in Corpus Christi. Serving in the army during World War I gave Perales the opportunity to advance professionally, but it also made him more aware of the racism that existed in the military and civilian worlds.

After the war, Perales became an employee of the U.S. Department of Commerce, which allowed him to get a Bachelor's degree at National University and a law degree in 1926. Perales embarked on a thirty-four year career in law, the diplomatic service, and civil rights. While running a thriving practice in South Texas, Perales served on numerous diplomatic missions throughout Latin America, gaining a global perspective on the problems of Mexican Americans. With Gonzales, Ben Garza, and state legislator J. T. Canales, Perales was one of the architects of LULAC. The path to equality and respect for Tejanos was, in Perales' opinion, through political and civic empowerment. This empowerment would be achieved through education and organization the goals of LULAC.

Perales also believed that native-born Tejanos and Mexican citizens had separate agendas and needed separate organizations to advance those agendas. "The Mexican-American citizen has rights by virtue of the natural laws of (the United States). The Mexican citizen, equally with other foreigners, has rights by virtue of well established international laws."[52]

Drawing on his expertise as a lawyer and a diplomat, Perales believed Mexicans and Mexican Americans were legally and constitutionally distinct identities. Tejanos and Mexicans, because of their citizenship, also had different ideologies; Mexicans cultivated Mexican cultural nationalism, while American citizens of Mexican descent desired the equal exercise of their rights as Americans. With Canales, Perales was the author of the LULAC constitution, whose provisions included a term limit for the LULAC president, a restriction on membership to U.S. citizens, and the establishment of English as LULAC's official language.[53] Alonso Perales saw the status of Mexican Americans in the broader context of Pan American relations, an opinion he shared with Dr. Carlos Castañeda, a LULAC supporter who was a professor of history at the University of Texas at Austin. A career in the U.S. diplomatic corps allowed Perales to have this international perspective and refined his own sense of identity. In fact, the name "League of United Latin American Citizens" was a reflection of a shared heritage between Tejanos and the population of the rest of Latin America.

Ironically, while later scholars would attempt to label the actions of Perales and LULAC as assimilating Mexican Americans into the broader American mainstream, he in fact desired to link the plight of the Tejano with that of other Latin Americans. He envisioned LULAC as a vanguard of Mexican Americans with the purpose of promoting "the political, social, and economic evolution of American citizens of Latin origin."[54]

Like Jefferson and Dubois, Perales proposed an educated and empowered class that would uplift the rest of the Mexican immigrant community. His methodology would be, in true progressive fashion, through education and the vote. Tejanos must be made aware of their rights as Americans, since Perales believed only American citizens could make use of those rights.

Perales was a widely published intellectual in the South Texas area. He articulated his ideology through several media; among these were two articles in *La Prensa* (ironically, an organ of Mexican nationalism)[55] written in 1927 and 1929. In them, he explained his motives for excluding Mexican citizens from the Tejano civil rights organization and defended himself from charges of excessive ambition and manipulation.

In 1937, Perales outlined his thought in the book *En Defensa De Mi Raza* (In Defense of My Race), a collection of articles, letters, and speeches describing the condition of Tejanos and his solutions. Education and unified organization were the answer for his people's oppressed situation. Written in Spanish but influenced by the cultural pluralism of John Dewey, the book concentrated on Perales' efforts in various situations where the rights of Tejanos were being threatened. He forcefully stated, "We consider ourselves to be aware Mexican-Americans [sic] from any point of view, as American as any other; and we challenge anyone to prove the contrary." Perales further argued, "We do not intend to disown our race. To the contrary, we feel very proud to carry Mexican blood in our veins. And it is not our proposal to ask, much less beg, Anglo-Saxons to permit us to mix with them socially. What we desire is progress, and that nothing should impede us from it. We want the rights and privileges we believe in to be respected. We desire equality of opportunity in the different arenas in the struggle for life, and equality before the courts of justice. In a word, we ask for justice and the opportunity for progress. There you have our objective. There you have our ideal."[56]

Interestingly, a large portion of both volumes cover the lobbying efforts of Perales and LULAC to have Mexican Americans classified as Caucasians for the purposes of the 1940 U.S. Census. An attempt by the Census Bureau to classify Tejanos as "persons of color" was seen as an insult.[57] Their protest was in one sense, prophetic, in that after the Second World War nearly all European immigrants would be absorbed into the racial rubric of white. The desire of Perales that Tejanos be linked with whites and European immigrants is particularly revealing about his concept of Tejano identity, given that Mexican-American activists in the nineteen sixties would reject the white designation and embrace their Indian heritage. Perales and the rest of LULAC desired to integrate Tejanos into the existing white political structures. He and other LULAC founders believed that only as Mexican Americans identified with white Texans would their rights and respect be secure, a view that would change after World War II.

New opportunities and injustices brought on by the post-war era prompted Perales to compile one of the most provocative and important books in the Mexican-American struggle for civil rights in 1948. The glaring contradiction of a nation fighting fascism and seeking the good will of Latin American countries—while at the same time treating the Mexicans within its borders as second-class citizens—is displayed in the work *Are We Good Neighbors?* An important shift in Perales' language, tone and approach to Anglo society can be detected in this book. Written to a general American audience in English, *Are We Good Neighbors?* proceeds from the assumption that the American identity of Tejanos was thoroughly established by their sacrificial service in the Armed forces during the war. Rights and equality are therefore no longer privileges to be requested hat in hand, but an entitlement to be demanded. In the manner of progressive muckrakers like Upton Sinclair or Lincoln Steffens (who attempted to destroy perceived injustices by exposing them) Perales compiled the statements of Tejano activists, Anglo liberals, and the affidavits of aggrieved Tejanos comprise the content of this compelling book.

As a Tejano entering the American political and diplomatic scene, Alonso Perales' thought reflected the tension between the Mexican communal tradition and the American individualistic tradition. His travels throughout the United States and Latin America allowed Perales to see the difficulties of the Tejano in the context of a pluralistic nation existing in an increasingly interdependent world. By identifying the problems of Mexican Americans with European immigrants, he eschewed the exceptionalism that Chicano activists would advance later. Perales did believe that Tejanos could preserve their culture while at the same time possessing the rights of Americans on an equal basis with Anglos. The members of LULAC would supply the leadership in that effort.

MANUEL C. GONZALES

No single life reflected the struggle within the Tejano mind more than Manuel C. Gonzales. Born in the Rio Grande Valley of Texas in October 1900, Gonzales was something of a prodigy. Despite being from an impoverished background, he was clerking at an Austin law firm by the age of 17, when he was also a founding member of La Liga Protectoria Mexicana (The Mexican Protective League), one of the earliest legal defense organizations for minorities. During the First World War, Gonzales was the secretary to the military attaché at the U.S. Embassy in Spain.[58] By 1924, he passed the bar exam.

Gonzales was involved in the cause of Tejano civil rights from a very early age. When the Mexican Protective League changed its goals in 1920, Gonzales joined the OSA. Later, he became disillusioned with the OSA leadership, and helped to found the Order Knights of America in February 1927.[59] Like Perales, Gonzales felt the only solution to "[t]he iniquitous exploitation" of Tejanos was in organization.[60]

It was here that Gonzales' life took a paradoxical turn. During the mid-twenties, he became secretary to the Mexican consul general in San Antonio, an arm of the Mexican government that was often engaged in controversy. Mexican citizens and Tejanos had often appealed to the consulate when their lives, property, and rights were at risk, with varying degrees of success. It was in the political and cultural interest of the consulate to maintain an ideology of Mexican nationalism and to encourage Mexican immigrants and their American-born children to return to Mexico. Lastly, the relationship of the consulate with the various elements of the Tejano community was directly affected by the Mexican Revolution and its aftermath. *La Prensa* as the voice of the exile elite class was vocal in its opinions for or against various Mexican administrations. For example, in late 1926, the president of Mexico was the anticlerical Plutarco Elias Calles, whose regime was detested by the conservative elite and middle class.[61]

M. C. Gonzales found himself in the vortex of competing agendas and emotions. At the same time, he relentlessly pursued this dream of creating a body that would provide Tejanos with legal protection, and would educate them on their rights as Texans and Americans. Gonzales' role as a founder of the OKA is also noteworthy because, unlike the Sons of America and later LULAC, the OKA did not exclude Mexican citizens from its membership.

According to Orozco, this may have arisen from Gonzales' ties to the consulate and his opinion that educated, middle-class Mexicans would be useful to the movement.[62] She also felt that Gonzales had probably favored the inclusion of Mexicans at the Harlingen convention, incurring the lasting distrust of Perales.[63] In an interview late in his life, Gonzales portrayed himself as allied with the Tejanos, a possible attempt to change his image historically.[64] Gonzales may have favored a united Mexican and Tejano organization, then changed his stance when events went against him. In any case, he became secretary at the LULAC founding convention in 1929, served as its president, and remained one of its major legal and intellectual voices for many decades thereafter.

Controversial choices in Gonzales' personal life were the final paradox of his career. After becoming an attorney, he married an Anglo woman and moved into a fashionable area of the Anglo North side of San Antonio.[65] Gonzales was criticized for seeming to abandon his ethnic heritage, the cardinal sin of "forgetting where he came from."

Whether these criticisms were valid or not (his second wife was a Tejana), Gonzales was probably willing to go much further than other Tejano activists in assimilating into Anglo Texan culture. Julie Lenninger Pycior noted that throughout the nineteen thirties, Gonzales had "warned against alliances with blacks."[66]

Nevertheless, Gonzales took the lead in attacking racial discrimination on the legal, organizational, and intellectual fronts. During his tenure as LULAC's president, the number of councils (local chapters) of LULAC was doubled.[67] He was also a lead attorney in a landmark case on school segregation, *Independent School District* v. *Salvatierra*.[68] Gonzales and LULAC tried unsuccessfully to end segregation of Tejano children in Del Rio, Texas public schools. However, he was effective in a pro bonum effort to prevent discrimination in South San Antonio schools.[69]

As did Perales, M.C. Gonzales wrote extensively on the condition of the Mexican American. In the *LULAC News,* the organizational newsletter, he wrote of Tejanos, "[a]lthough American citizens, the same as any other citizen of Cosmopolitan America, yet . . . he is looked upon not as an integral part of his native country, with the unquestioned right to enjoy the many privileges that citizens of the United States are given . . . but he is in many places called an alien." Continuing, Gonzales addressed his remarks to potential LULAC members about their identity: "[y]ou don't belong to Mexico, and the Anglo-Saxon will not accept you socially, politically, in the public schools, in restaurants, picture shows, dances, and many other places. You were born here, yet you are not generally accepted where you were born or where you are living."[70]

With Perales, Gonzales believed that the solution to the plight of Tejanos was organization, education, and direct but peaceful protest. He declared that LULAC was "organized to fight for our legal rights as citizens of this country upon the principles outlined in our constitution."[71]

Through the educational system, Gonzales and the other LULAC founders were deeply influenced by the progressive ideology of their time. A belief in progress, in the ability of humanity to manipulate its environment, a desire both for social justice and social control, and a conviction that education can be used as an instrument to socialize persons into new ways of behavior were foundational to their thinking.

Gonzales, Perales, and the South Texas Tejano middle class wanted to educate the community to think and act in a way that would command respect from the majority Anglos. While they both had a passionate desire for equal rights and social justice, they preferred the controlled atmosphere of courts, legislatures, and schools for their battlegrounds, avoiding direct protests. These sentiments were displayed in the LULAC constitution whose first aim was "To develop within the members of our race the best, purest, and most perfect type of a true and loyal citizen of the United States of America."[72]

Tejanos found themselves in a culture that excluded them from political power, segregated their children out of Anglo public schools, and consigned the entire race to the lowest rungs of the Texas economy and society. The response to this discrimination occurred in stages, corresponding to Tejanos' changing self-identity. In the late nineteenth and early twentieth centuries, Tejanos formed mutual aid societies and appealed to the Mexican consulates to address injustices against them. In doing so, they were responding as temporary residents in a foreign land, i.e., as Mexicans.

After the First World War, middle class Tejanos formed the OSA and similar groups that were patterned after ethnically specific entities of European immigrants and German residents of San Antonio. While the OSA retained many of the benefits of the *mutualistas*, it was increasingly American in its practices. Rituals resembled those of American Masonic Lodges, and the OSA's membership and social milieu de-emphasized the role of women. Lastly, it also began to seek legal and social equality for Tejanos through the American legal system. Overall, bodies like the OSA reflected the growing awareness of Tejanos as American citizens.

LULAC represented a final stage in this changing consciousness. Alonso Perales, Manuel C. Gonzales, and the other founders of this new organization restricted membership to American citizens only, excluding Mexicans, and made English the official language of LULAC. Their ideology was individualistic and progressive. Although women's and youth auxiliaries were created, they had no leadership role in the overall structure. The communal bent of the mutual aid societies was abandoned in favor of individual empowerment through civic education for adults and equal access to public school education for children. Arming the Tejano with the tools for success in the liberal U.S. society was the main aim of LULAC.

This ideology was reflected in the writings of Perales and Gonzales. In spite of their apparent agreement, the two men were in constant conflict. It began when Gonzales favored the inclusion of Mexican citizens in the fledgling civil rights movement, which Perales opposed. Their rivalry continued when the San Antonio LULAC Council split in the early thirties, and was fueled by the dilemma between the desire to hold onto Mexican communal social patterns, as Perales did, and the tendency toward social as well as political integration, reflected in the life of Gonzales. Given that their values would ultimately triumph over the Mexican nationalism of *La Prensa*, their feud seems ironic and unfortunate.

By 1960, however, Richard Garcia could see a profound change in identity, that "LULAC had forged a new mentality . . . and it was a hegemonic ideological and psychological bond: the acceptance of Americanism, liberalism and patriotism."[73] With the emergence of a native middle class created by the prosperity of the interwar period, a new mindset and organization also emerged. Increasingly the community embraced the liberal ideologies of participatory democracy, free market capitalism (coupled with an emphasis on the Protestant work ethic), and yearned to be an unhindered participant in that system. In turn, the new identity among Mexican Americans encouraged them to think in terms of the Emersonian "Party of Hope" and "The Party of the Future."[74] This ideology of Emerson valued individualism, rather than tradition.

The values of LULAC's creators formed within a context of middle class, liberal ideals. These were shaped in the environments of emerging progressivism, a conservative Mexican intellectual heritage, and an equally conservative southern social structure. On the other hand, the setting of California, where the largest population of Mexican Americans lived, was profoundly different from that of San Antonio and South Texas.

Chapter Three

Another Community: Identity among Working Class Mexican Americans, 1935–1941

The voices of LULAC and *La Prensa* were not the only representatives of the Tejano community in San Antonio in the 1929–1949 era. These were in fact a minority of the impoverished city within the city. In the view of social historian Juliet Kirk Blackwelder, the plight of this majority was made worse by the Great Depression. "A privileged few passed through the Depression in ease, but overall San Antonians suffered more then did most other city dwellers."[1]

However, the near collapse of San Antonio's economy did not drastically affect Tejano cultural identity or result in a change of representative intellectuals. The southern general consensus and Tejano middle-class consensus remained in place. The causes for this are many, and include reforms on the part of New Deal liberals, the lack of a pervasive campaign of repatriation against the Tejanos, and the lack of a strong labor movement.

Conditions were vastly different at the same time in Southern California, where Mexican-American intellectual and political energy was directed primarily toward economic concerns, such as labor movements and political groups oriented toward the left end of the political spectrum. Participants were more likely to be members of the lower classes and more likely to be women. These groups were the intellectual precursors of the Chicano movement of the 1960s, in the same way the Popular Front of the thirties gave way to the New Left of the Baby Boomer Generation. In Texas, there were efforts to center Tejano political action on questions of economic inequity. Most notable among these was the Pecan Shellers' Strike of the late thirties and the leadership of young radical Emma Tenayuca. In spite of her magnetism among the pecan shellers (nearly all of whom were women), Tenayuca found herself unwanted by the mainstream labor movement at the same time that organized labor found a hostile climate in San Antonio. Although the pecan shellers won initial victories for higher wages, federally mandated wage laws and the mechanization of pecan shelling resulted in the loss of their jobs. Their attempts to organize San Antonio's Tejano work force were stymied.

The only successful grass-roots movement in Texas during the thirties was the Liga Pro-Defensa Escuelar (School Defense League), a broad based coalition set up to protest the unequal educational conditions for Tejano children. The history and makeup of this group are informative in understanding the change in Tejano identity after World War II.

What emerged from the war were two Mexican-American communities—one in South Texas, the other in Southern California—that both had faced discrimination, but in fact developed from different environments and had divergent experiences. From these would emerge two differing notions of Mexican-American identity.

EMMA AND THE PECAN SHELLERS

Emma Tenayuca saw herself as an American involved in the larger struggle of workers for justice in the midst of the Depression. With the rest of the Old Left, she felt that her struggle was based upon American ideals, although it crossed national boundaries. Like many others, she believed that her activism in the Communist Party was in a tradition that stretched backed to the American Revolution.

The Great Depression hit the economy of San Antonio with terrible force, putting thousands out of work. The temporary nature of city's two major industries (tourism and the military) left it with few economic resources to combat the downturn.[2] Conditions were especially difficult for Tejano men who traditionally worked in low skilled jobs. Men had to compete with women for positions in unsanitary, unhealthy, and tedious labor. Work relief in New Deal agencies such as the Works Progress Administration was closed to unemployed non-citizens, making their lives all the more desperate.

Tejanos lived in shacks of tin and cardboard with no indoor plumbing, making them vulnerable to diseases like tuberculosis and infantile diarrhea. These conditions were being only partially addressed by liberal advocates–on the national scene by Eleanor Roosevelt and locally by congressman and Mayor Maury Maverick. The American Federation of Labor organized only skilled labor and shied away from unionizing minorities.

The American Communist Party, more specifically its Popular Front, attempted to fill this political vacuum through the creation of advocacy groups for unskilled industrial labor, agricultural workers, tenant farmers, and racial minorities. Among Mexican-Americans, this was manifested in the Workers' Alliance in Texas and the Congress of Spanish Speaking Peoples, primarily in California. In both cases, the movements were organized and energized by idealistic Mexican-American women, Josefina Fierro de Bright in Los Angeles and Emma Tenayuca in San Antonio.

Tenayuca was born in 1916 in San Antonio, Texas in a family of 11 children. Even as a child she could recall hearing political discussions among her family and being taken to political gatherings. "I started going to the Plaza and political rallies when I was only six or seven years old. That's where I learned to sing. I learned the anarchist words to the Marseille. You had the influence of [sic] Flores Magon brothers."[3]

In high school Tenayuca became involved in discussion groups with fellow students in the depths of the Great Depression. Upon graduation, she went to observe the striking workers at the Fink Cigar Company. She commented, "I had a basic underlying faith in the idea of freedom and fairness. I felt that there was something that had to be done. But the idea of having women kicked (which the local sheriff threatened to do) now, that was something I was going to do something about, and I went to out on the picket line. That was the first time I was arrested."[4]

From her involvement in the cigar strike, Tenayuca joined the Workers' Alliance, a Popular Front group seeking to organize workers in the agriculturally-based industries. Richard Garcia asserted that San Antonio's development in the mid-twentieth century was due to industrialization. He is partly mistaken, because that industry was dependent on agriculture and the military bases of the city. The low-wage jobs that these produced retarded the city's long-term growth. Because of this, San Antonio dropped in population from the largest Texas city in 1920 to the third largest.[5]

Tenayuca and the Workers Alliance became involved with the strike at the Southern Pecan Shelling Company, which had lowered its wages for its mostly female work force. A study by the Works Progress Administration discovered "The pecan shelling industry in San Antonio is concentrated for the most part on the West Side of the city [sic]. In this area of about 4 square miles . . . live at least 65,000 of San Antonio's estimated 100,000 Mexicans. Here also is one of the most extensive slums to be found in any American city, with decrepit wooden shacks in crowded 'courts' overflowing with Mexican families who are forced by poverty to live there."[6] The labor actions contrasted with the work of LULAC in that it was primarily female and focused on the city's laboring classes. Blackwelder observed that nearly all the labor unrest in the thirties occurred in San Antonio's lowest-paying industries and that in them "Mexican-American women predominated and consequently they were the driving force behind strikes in the formation of labor organizations."[7]

Emma Tenayuca emerged as the leading organizer and inspirational figure of the strike. Due to her fiery and passionate speeches, the strikers labeled her La Pasionaria. She had joined the Communist Party in 1937 and married its state chairman, Homer Brooks. After she and thousands of strikers were jailed, and local police broke up picket lines with tear gas, the pecan shellers were successful in getting a raise. With the passage of the Fair Labor Standards Act Of 1938, a minimum-wage was mandated for all industry, but the law's unintended impact was to replace low-paid "hand-work businesses" with machinery.[8]

Tenayuca's definitive statement on identity came in an article co-authored with Homer Brooks in the radical journal *The Communist*. In the article, "The Mexican Question in the Southwest," the authors gave a historical survey of the region that concluded, "We can the state that the Spanish-speaking population of the Southwest, both the American-born and the foreign-born, are one people." Tenayuca further explained, "The Mexican population of the Southwest is closely bound together by historical, political, and cultural ties."[9] Utilizing classical Marxist analysis, Tenayuca saw Mexican Americans as an exploited people (restricted to low-wage labor) in an exploited region. According to her, "The treatment meted out to the Mexicans as whole has from the earliest days of the sovereignty of the United States been that of the conquered people."[10]

Mexican Americans, according to Tenayuca, were oppressed in all aspects of life: social, educational, political, and economic. However, her solutions were consistent with those of the Popular Front nationally, and refuted any cultural separatism as would be evident later in the Chicano movement. In her article she elaborates, "Should the conclusion be drawn that the Mexican people in the Southwest, constitute a nation—or that they form a segment of the Mexican nation? Our view is no." Tenayuca concluded by saying, "We must accordingly regard the Mexican people in the Southwest as part of the American nation, who however, have not been so accepted by the American bourgeoisie; the latter has continued to hinder the process of national unification of the American people by treating the Mexican and Spanish-Americans as a conquered people."[11]

Tenayuca's desire was the integration of Mexican Americans with other ethnic groups, the same "process of national unification" that was the goal of mainstream liberalism and groups such as LULAC. A cultural shift by LULAC away from an exclusively American focus was welcomed by Tenayuca, who said "This important organization of the Mexican middle-class will play an increasing role in the general movement for Mexican rights."[12] Her approach was consistent with that of the Old Left during the late nineteen thirties, to be as inclusive as possible, and at least to appear to forsake revolution for reform. Arthur Koestler wrote of this period, "All revolutionary slogans, references to class struggle and the Dictatorship of the Proletariat were in one sweep relegated to the lumber room. They were replaced by a brand new façade . . . called 'Popular Front for Peace and against Fascism.' Its doors were wide open to all men of good will, Social-ists, Catholics, Conservatives, Nationalists."[13]

The National Congress of Spanish-speaking Peoples also applied this approach to Mexican-American civil rights. The Congress was an umbrella organization founded in California by, among others, Josefina Fierro de Bright, the wife of radical playwright John Bright. In 1939 the Congress attempted to sponsor a national gathering of activists at the University of

New Mexico on March 24 of that year. Persons as diverse as Tenayuca (who mentioned the Congress in her article),[14] and members of LULAC were invited to the upcoming meeting. Mario Garcia noted that, "The *Albuquerque Journal* remarked on a broad spectrum of sponsors of the national convention. These included Maury Maverick, ex-congressman from San Antonio; Melvyn Douglas of the Screen Actors Guild; J. F. Zimmerman, President of the University of New Mexico; Oliver Wright, organizer for the New Mexico Federation of Labor; Carlos Castañeda of the University of Texas; Donald Henderson, national president of UCAPAWA; George Soule, member of the editorial staff of the *New Republic;* Paul S. Taylor of the University Of California; and writer Waldo Frank. Moreover, several artists and writers, especially from Hollywood, joined in the appeal for the Albuquerque convention. Among these were Upton Sinclair, Herbert Biberman of the Screen Directors Guild, And John Bright of the League of American Writers." It would have been the first truly national meeting on the subject of Mexican-American civil rights. However, when the Congress's Communist sponsorship was discovered, the more moderate participants declined to attend, and the University refused to sponsor the event. This failed attempt at co-optation reduced the Congress to a radical, California-based movement.[15]

The inclusive environment of the Popular Front allowed Tenayuca and others to enter the Communist Party and participate in its affiliated organizations without having to enter the Kafkaesque underworld experienced by Richard Wright, Whitaker Chambers, and earlier participants in the Old Left. In fact, Tenayuca's ultimate goals as a party member, labor organizer, and intellectual were not that different from those of LULAC, i.e., the economic and political integration of Tejanos with the rest of American society.

The Nazi-Soviet Non-aggression Pact of August 23, 1939 was the reef that the Popular Front was dashed upon. It was an ideological about-face by Russia after a steady stream of anti-fascist propaganda throughout the decade. "I don't think" Tenayuca later recalled, "there was a communist in the country who wasn't puzzled."[16] In an attempt to reconcile the apparent contradictions, she and other San Antonio Communists gathered in a room in San Antonio's Municipal Auditorium after the treaty's signing. The meeting precipitated a riot led by militant anti-communists and others opposed to the Nazi regime. From this altercation Tenayuca barely escaped injury, but the experience caused her to leave political and labor activity permanently.

Tenayuca was like many independent-thinking individuals who joined the Communist Party in the twenties and thirties but left when they could no longer follow the Stalinist line after 1939. The horrors of Communism, with its destruction of individual freedoms and cynical diplomacy repelled many in the Popular Front. The loss of idealism and energy of Tenayuca's generation was lamentable. Had it been spent in a better cause, it might have saved the world and nation much misery. It speaks poorly of the political environment of the time that Tenayuca, Richard Wright, and others had no other avenues to address the real injustices that existed.

MARIA L. HERNANDEZ AND THE SCHOOL IMPROVEMENT LEAGUE

Education had been the keystone of all LULAC's efforts to improve the condition of Tejanos and create a Mexican-American consciousness. The development of their advocacy was embodied in La Liga Pro Defensa Escolar, organized in 1934 by Eleutrio Escobar, a LULAC member, along with 73 other Mexican-American organizations. The methods of La Liga (later known as the School Improvement League) reflected a change in identity among San Antonio's middle-class leadership. The League began as a collective effort by LULAC and other Tejano groups to promote the improvement of education in San Antonio's Spanish-speaking community. It reflected a belief that education was the only avenue of betterment for the children of the city's most impoverished areas, a value central to the American ideology of self-improvement.

In 1934, the League operated as a Mexican organization. Its newsletter, name and constitution were in Spanish. The immediate goal of the league at its founding was the improvement of existing "Mexican" schools,[17] not the integration of Tejano children into Anglo schools. The new body sought educational opportunity for Mexican Americans, but on their own terms as Mexicans.

This was borne out at an October 24 rally that over 10,000 residents attended, mostly women and children.[18] It was also attended by representatives of all the League's sponsoring organizations, including virtually all of the Tejano leadership in the city and South Texas. Among these was Maria L. Hernandez, who in 1929 founded La Orden Caballeros de America (Order Knights Of America). Hernandez and her husband Pedro created the Caballeros for the purpose of improving the educational and social condition of Tejanos, but on Mexican cultural terms. Spanish was the functional language of the organization and its vision was hemispheric. The cultural and intellectual inclusion of all Americans as equals was its aim, as stated by its slogan *Americanismo es nuestro* (Americanism is ours)[19]. The fate of the Tejano was tied, according to Hernandez, with their fellow Latin Americans to the south. Her outlook was further exemplified in a 1945 essay on Mexican political and family relations.[20] In 1970 Hernandez continued her lifelong activism by speaking in support of La Raza Unida Party, the political wing of the Chicano Movement in Texas. Her thinking and activism emphasized the identity of the Tejano as a Pan American citizen, belonging to many nations but possessing a distinct culture. This contrasted with the efforts and exertions of LULAC to make Mexican Americans into the best citizens of the U.S. However, Hernandez cooperated with LULAC in its attempts to improve education for children in San Antonio's predominantly Mexican-American West Side.

The shape and direction of that movement were changing, however. In 1935 the Liga ended its activity for seemingly unknown reasons, but personal and organizational rivalries within San Antonio's LULAC chapters certainly contributed.[21] The stresses of the Depression and World War II also may have caused the stoppage. In 1947 the group reconstituted itself under Escobar's leadership under the name of the School Improvement League. Arguing that it was fighting for the rights of Americans,[22] the League was now bilingual, integrationist, and at the same time more militant. This shift in focus and tone was reflected in all minority intellectuals and activists as the result of America's successful war against fascism. Also, the League was under the control of a new, younger brand of leaders such as future Congressman Henry B. Gonzalez and attorney Gustavo Garcia. Born in Texas, this generation felt that their service in the Second World War entitled them to all the rights and benefits of other Americans. When the League elected Garcia to the San Antonio school board, passed a bond issue for improvements, and closed down the most dangerous and dilapidated school buildings, its new militancy bore fruit.

Gus Garcia was typical of many Tejanos in his generation who saw their status in the context of America's new role of leadership in the postwar world. At a 1952 testimonial dinner given in his honor he said, "I say to you that if we could only make a determined effort to cleanse these moral ulcers of racial and economic discrimination, these outmoded concepts of personal superiority over less fortunate folk . . . we can then assume our newly found position of leadership among other free nations of the earth without fear of reproach or danger of repulsion."[23] Earlier, Garcia also prophesied the future course of Mexican-American civil-rights when he said, "It appears to me that our task consists first and foremost of ironing out the kinks in our democratic form of government beginning on a local level and then proceed upward to a state and national stratum."[24]

Garcia's life was a tragic case of what might have been. Valedictorian of his high school class, he graduated from the University of Texas and received a degree from its law school. During the Second World War, Garcia served in the judge advocate Corps in the Pacific, and was present during the founding of the United Nations in 1945.[25] According to printer Ruben Mungia and Garcia's legal colleague Carlos Cadena, the attorney possessed an intellect unequaled by any Mexican American in modern history.[26] Gus Garcia was a lead attorney in *Delgado* vs. *Bastrop I.S.D.*, a 1948 case that outlawed segregation of Mexican-American children in Texas public schools. The zenith of Garcia's career came in *Hernandez v. Texas* in 1954,[27] where he argued before the Supreme Court that the historical exclusion of Mexican Americans from Texas juries violated the U.S. Constitution. Garcia's star appeared to be on the rise when he became an acquaintance of Lyndon Johnson and John Kennedy.

By the mid-1950s, however, serious alcoholism began to undermine the promising career of Gus Garcia. In the late sixties, when President Johnson considered appointing a Mexican-American to the U.S. Supreme Court, Garcia would have been the perfect candidate. Sadly, in 1964 Garcia was discovered dead on a San Antonio park bench, the result of alcohol-induced seizures.[28]

At the beginning of the post-World War II era, San Antonio's Mexican-American community identified itself increasingly with a middle-class leadership that perceived its identity in American terms. Service in war armed Tejanos with the conviction that they were the equals of their Anglo counterparts and would demand to be treated as such.

Labor and radical movements found San Antonio to be inhospitable to their activism. The southern anti-union climate of the general community, combined with the largely antirevolutionary roots of much of Tejano elite (i.e., *La Prensa*) produced a conservative atmosphere that muffled other voices. Richard Garcia observed, "Regardless of strikes and union activities, San Antonio was not becoming a union town. Consequently, the consciousness and ideology of the Mexican worker was more closely tied to the ideology of the Mexican-American middle class . . . than to a union or workers consciousness."[29] Venturing as to the underlying cause for this, Garcia said, "Because of the city's economic constituencies (military, retail, agriculture and tourism) the political climate and ideology of the political elites were always skewed to the right."[30]

In addition, because of the war and the consequent exposure of Tejanos to American culture, Mexican reference points slowly began to lose their hold. The circulation of *La Prensa* declined during the forties and fifties as the community gravitated toward San Antonio's two English language newspapers. And although Maria L. Hernandez would continue her activism, its Mexican bent would not attract followers until the nineteen sixties.

The environment of San Antonio stood in sharp contrast to that of Los Angeles, the only city in the United States with a larger Mexican-American population. The political, economic, and historical milieu of Southern California produced an entirely different identity within its Mexican-American neighborhoods. Instead of forming a well-defined niche that allowed them to strive for life as Americans, Mexican Americans in California perceived their identity to be under siege. Chicanos found little or no historical presence to ground them in their new homeland, at the same time that their culture and history were being attacked. Also, California was more receptive to radical movements in both labor and politics, and Mexican Americans were part of these efforts. All of these factors would combine to produce a very different community identity than existed in San Antonio.

Chapter Four

A City of Migrants: Los Angeles and Chicano Identity

One afternoon in San Antonio, a judge asked lawyer and LULAC president Jimmy Tafolla, "Why there were some Mexicans who resented being called 'Mexicans'?"

Jimmy promptly answered, "Judge, I'm going to give you a bit of back history, and then answer your question by asking you a question. My great-grandfather was a native-born American citizen: my grandfather was a native-born American citizen; so was my father; so am I, and so are my children. Five generations of native-born citizens of this country. Now, do you think that my children ought to be called 'Mexicans'?"

The old judge just smiled and said, "I guess you're right Jimmy."[1]

This story demonstrates the sense of historical groundedness felt by Mexican Americans of San Antonio, a sense that would be lacking among the immigrants of southern California, the largest group of Mexicans in the United States. Living as disconnected strangers, California Chicanos had no sense of the identity as Americans that anchored their cousins in Texas. As a result, when they were victims of discrimination and forced assimilation, they had no sense of identity to fall back on.

Reviewing the Californian historical experience, Richard Griswold del Castillo poignantly observed that "In the sixteenth century the early Spanish explorers believed that California was an island. It is well known that the very name 'California' is derived from the old European legend of the Amazon Queen Califa who ruled an island kingdom somewhere in the Orient." He then concluded, "In many ways southern California remains a mythical island in the historical and cultural experience of the North American mind. Historical interpretations of the experiences of the Mexican-origin population in this area of United States have been influenced by the development of southern California as a distinctive region within United States."[2]

45

An economy of industry and commercial agriculture caused the state of California to grow at a phenomenal rate during the early decades of the twentieth century. The new economy induced immigration from both the Midwestern U.S. and Mexico that further fueled this growth. George J. Sanchez remarked that California's fluid culture created an identity crisis among the entire population. Speaking of the Anglos, he noted that "Their own mobility prompted the concern to define better the new culture in which they found themselves. But stressing conformity to the American industrial order, they could try to impose stability on a society in rapid flux."[3]

During the same time that Anglos were moving westward, thousands of Mexican migrants came north as a result of the Revolution in Mexico. Because of the upheaval in their country, these new immigrants added to the cultural turbulence in California. Meanwhile, progressivism emerged in the U.S. as an ideal that society could be remolded through education and reform. One of the major objects of this reform was assimilating European immigrants into American society. Reformers on the West Coast felt the same thing could be accomplished for the Mexican immigrants. The chief goal of progressive ideology in California became to socialize recently arrived Mexicans and their children to think and act as Americans. A program was therefore developed that had the effect of denigrating Mexican language and culture, and ultimately, their sense of identity.

Observing this acculturation program, Griswold del Castillo believed that Mexican immigrants in California were more vulnerable than their Texas counterparts. He said, "It seems more likely that these urbanized Chicanos were under more pressure to assimilate than their rural cousins in Texas . . . since their identity was less tied to being born and raised in the region."[4]

The ideology of progressivism, with its twin concerns for social justice and social control, had very different impacts on Mexican Americans in California and in Texas. In San Antonio, middle-class Mexican Americans attempted to employ education as a tool to socialize the community about its rights as American citizens, addressing the problems of discrimination and poverty. It was progressivism within a Mexican context, defined by Mexicans.

In California, progressivism was wielded by Anglos as an instrument of social control to assimilate Mexican immigrants into a dominant culture. Governmental institutions that Anglos created relating to immigration reflected this. For example, Sanchez observed that "Progressives in California established the Commission on Immigration and Housing in 1913, and it became an instrument for Americanizing Mexican immigrants."[5] In fact, Ricardo Romo discovered that the Commission underwent a metamorphosis from its early years as a social advocacy group for Mexican immigrants to being the main governmental body in charge of the Americanization program, pressing for the restriction of further immigration.[6]

Although humanitarian in its intent, the goal of the Commission and similar programs was to make immigrants indistinguishable from other Americans. Educators, business, and social service agencies were to carry out this pervasive program. Discouraging or even penalizing the use of Spanish in school, altering patterns of dress and child rearing became the main practices of Anglo progressives in "reforming" the Mexican immigrant community. Whatever the intent, the result was to create a sense of shame among Mexicans for their cultural differences. The detrimental consequences reverberated down through to the present, and the lives of Chicanos like Richard Rodriguez and Kevin Johnson were often permanently scarred. Rodriguez wrote of how his self-esteem was damaged by the comments of his mother and other women in his family, who were very likely influenced by the culture around them. "Simply, I judged myself ugly. And, since the women in my family had been the ones who discussed it in such worried tones, I felt my dark skin made me unattractive to women. I grew divorced from my body."[7]

The Americanization program's intellectual center was located at the University of Southern California, a college founded largely by recently-arrived Methodists. Directed by Professor Emory Bogardus, the assimilation program had both sociological and religious roots, as noted by George J. Sanchez. "What distinguished the efforts made by USC . . . was its heavily moralistic impetus, which had no qualms about mixing Protestant sensibilities, academic research, and public policy."[8] Sanchez went further by asserting that the program of reformers at USC was counterproductive and destructive to Chicano culture. He argued that the reformers "understood full well that despite the range of motivations behind Americanization, the price of acceptance for Mexicans into American society via their programs was predicated on the abandonment of a culture they perceived as inherently inferior."[9]

Interestingly, the USC mindset contrasted with progressive settlement workers in large northeastern cities like Chicago, home of millions of new immigrants from Europe. Discussing their attitudes, Allen F. Davis stated, "[T]he settlement worker's greatest contribution lay . . . in its insisting that immigrants preserve the customs and traditions of the old country, assuring immigrants that it was not necessary to reject the past to become Americans. Settlement workers appreciated the fact that for many immigrants, the process of Americanization was harsh and often meant ripping out the beliefs of a lifetime."[10] Attitudes of cultural superiority also pervaded Anglo Americans' relations with Native Americans in the West.[11]

In spite of the programs in California, the continual influx of Mexican immigrants and their concentration into barrios such as East Los Angeles perpetuated Mexican values within the community, preventing the transformation desired by reformers. Sanchez believed that this failure "led to an institutional structure in education that relegated the Chicano to menial labor and second-class citizenship."[12] The educational system of California tended to route Mexican Americans into low-paying jobs, but more importantly it downgraded their culture and their language. Instead of being seen as an instrument of individual and community uplift, California's schools were perceived by Mexicans as an instrument of Anglo domination and exclusion.

REPATRIATION AND THE ZOOT SUIT RIOTS

While European immigrants may have encountered discrimination, language barriers, and other difficulties Mexican Americans shouldered the additional burden of being seen as an inferior race because of the color of their skin, their Native American lineage, and legacy of defeat from the Mexican War. In California, this was tragically displayed during the nineteen thirties and forties through repeated acts of discrimination which they suffered. These had a direct bearing on their community's leadership, and were the determining factor in preventing the Mexican immigrant community from developing an American consciousness. The Depression saw the organized deportation or repatriation of Mexicans (and in many cases their American-born children) in southern California. During World War II, tensions between Navy personnel and Chicano youths exploded into violence in what became known as the Zoot Suit Riots in 1943. The immigrant community felt itself marked out as outsiders who provided only the menial labor that Americans refused to do themselves. They consequently believed that the American dream was closed to them.

Although Mexican-American residents of Texas faced daily discrimination and were often the objects of repatriation, Griswold del Castillo noted that their historical ties to the land anchored their identity as Texans and Americans.[13] Also, the Second World War created an expansion of the San Antonio military infrastructure, and Tejanos participated in the resulting prosperity. The two communities therefore continued down different paths.

Throughout the 1920s, Mexicans in California experienced consistent discrimination in jobs, housing, and education. Bogardus discovered that realtors who attempted to sell homes to Mexican immigrants in traditionally Anglo neighborhoods met with angry resistance.[14] He also found that whatever their education, Chicanos were permanently trapped in low-paying jobs. This discouraged immigrants from applying for U.S. citizenship.[15]

Discrimination took on organized proportions in 1931, when the full brunt of the Depression began to be felt in southern California, and Anglos were laid off from their skilled positions. Soon they competed with Mexicans for lower wage jobs, and a coordinated campaign was begun to send the immigrants back to Mexico, in a fashion similar to the repatriation of Japanese Americans to the United States interior ten years later.

Government officials in California insisted that Mexican immigrants were becoming a burden on the public welfare rolls, and were leaving the country willingly. But evidence pointed to the probability that many emp-loyed Mexicans, as well as U.S. citizens of Mexican descent, were forced to leave on free Southern Pacific trains by various means of intimidation. In describing this melancholy exodus, Carey McWilliams noted that immi-grants seemed to suffer few ill effects from the repatriation, but their children were traumatized. He reported that "A friend of mine who was recently in Mazatlan . . . found a young Mexican girl on one of the southbound trains crying because she had to leave Belmont High School."[16]

Intellectually the impact on the Mexican community of southern California was twofold. First it cemented their identity as foreigners who were accepted only for their labor. Sanchez inquired, "What historians of repa-triation have not yet examined is how the loss of thousands of family mem-bers, friends, and neighbors affected the social identity of those individuals who stayed in United States."[17]

Additionally, repatriation deprived Chicanos of community leadership at a crucial stage in its development, effectively decapitating it.[18] The most destructive characteristic of this phenomenon was that it was both rural and urban and cut across class lines.[19] Texas repatriation was mainly rural and did not impact San Antonio significantly.[20]

The ambivalence of Chicanos toward their status as Americans was exacerbated during the "Zoot Suit Riots" on June 3–13, 1943 in East Los Angeles. The city had become a major training and dispersal point for thousands of soldiers, sailors and Marines. Many of these bases were in the heart of the Mexican-American community. Psychologist Mauricio Magón theorized that the tensions and isolation brought about by military life caused the servicemen to "let off steam" by attacking Mexican-American youths, whose flamboyant clothing set them apart as nonconformists. Mexican-American teenagers had for weeks been demonized in the local newspapers as delinquents, further isolating them from wartime society. Magón charged, "At least for ten days in southern California and on some adjoining bases, the military lost control of several thousand servicemen."[21]

For the Mexican-American community of Los Angeles, the riots appeared to be one more example of American society turning against them (at the time when thousands of Mexican Americans were serving in the U.S. military). Manuel Gonzales eloquently drove this home when he said, "For many Mexicans . . . the Zoot Suit Riots, like the repatriation of the 1930s, left a scar which never completely healed. The events of the 1930s and 1940s go a long way in explaining the disaffection of the Mexican population with the dominant society and government. For years and years, even among those who were citizens of United States would see and identify themselves as 'Mexicans' not 'Americans.'"[22]

Another determining factor inhibiting Chicano identity was the urban, ahistorical environment of Los Angeles itself. George J. Sanchez believed that "Los Angeles provided Mexican immigrants more latitude than any other community in the southwest in shaping a Mexican-American identity."[23] The evidence seems to conclude exactly the opposite. In fact, it was the very anonymity and lack of historical connection that made it very difficult for Mexicans in Los Angeles to form their own identity. The city attempted to stamp its own identity on them, a reality that separated Chicanos from their Tejano cousins more than any other.

Among many other intellectuals, Theodore Drieser has commented that the vastness of urban life made it possible for individuals to reinvent themselves there according to the needs and desires of the moment. Yet what is also often noted is the way the city shapes those who dwell in it. Thomas Bender has commented on a crucial role that the life of the city has played on the life of the mind. This was particularly the case with Los Angeles, a city described as "having no center"—no fixed, defining point of reference from which all else radiated, as was the Alamo in San Antonio. The rise of Los Angeles from relative obscurity at the beginning of the twentieth century, populated by people who jettisoned their past, added to the city's lack of a true historical presence. Griswold del Castillo also pointed out that "the vast majority of Chicanos have no historical memory of land ownership in [California]" and as a result, "there just is not the same kind of long-term community bonding and identification that has occurred in the small . . . towns in New Mexico, Colorado, and Texas."[24]

Thus, the city's identity was shaped by whoever could command its intellectual resources, such as newspapers, the universities, and the local Chamber of Commerce. All of these were dominated by Anglo immigrants from the Midwest who sought to mold everything into a secularized, Protestant, pro-business image.[25] In contrasting the two regions, Sanchez noted, "For both Anglos and Mexicans in California, life was constantly on the move. In Texas, conditions were more settled and traditional."[26] Variations in historical and social experiences between Chicanos and Tejanos mirrored those between blacks in the urban North and the rural South.

UNIONISM AND THE SPANISH-SPEAKING CONGRESS

The creation of a labor movement, supported and received among the larger community, was still another important distinction between California and Texas. Although labor and radical groups faced determined opposition in both states, during the Great Depression, activists in California found support from journalists, literary figures, and the motion picture industry. According to Anne Loftis, labor organizers and radicals "had considerable success among Hollywood actors, producers, and screenwriters who felt guilty to be earning weekly salaries in four figures while farm workers were paid fifteen cents an hour."[27] Left-of-center activists working to improve conditions on labor-intensive farms and among longshoremen operated from a larger critical culture from which they drew ideological and man-power support. Loftis commented that "the Old Left in California was a motley collection of 'professional people, intellectuals, and students who had no connection with agriculture,' who supported labor strikes led by the Communist Party."[28]

The most dramatic working-out of this in the Mexican-American community was the Congress of Spanish-Speaking Peoples, one of the many left-wing organizations that benefited from the help provided by well-to-do activists. One of its founders was Josefina Fierro de Bright, wife of playwright John Bright. Fierro de Bright founded the Congress in Los Angeles in 1938 with labor organizer Luisa Moreno and liberal political activist Eduardo Quevedo.[29] As mentioned earlier, the Congress attempted to unite all Mexican-American groups nationwide, a desire that was frustrated in March 1939 when its Popular Front connections were exposed.[30] Thereafter the focus of the Congress' activism was in California. Its activism on behalf of Mexican citizens and its willingness to work with African Americans set the Congress apart from LULAC. In the spring of 1939 it successfully opposed the Swing bill in the California Legislature that would have blocked unemployment relief to Mexican nationals. The Congress also protested the removal of "Mexicans and blacks from relief as being unworthy of assistance."[31] Similar actions showed that the Congress saw Mexicans and Mexican Americans as a single group working with other minorities for their rights. Influenced by Marxism and Progressive liberalism, their identity as American reformers was more cosmopolitan than that of LULAC.

Both Marxism and reform liberalism characterized modern society as interdependent, an attitude reflected in the thinking of Emma Tenayuca and the Congress Of Spanish-Speaking Peoples. The founding ideology of LULAC however, spoke of individual rights and self improvement, the doctrines of preindustrial and rural America. This difference in ideology foreshadowed the conflict and that would occur among Tejanos in the nineteen sixties.

Between 1939 and 1941, the Congress attempted to negotiate the twists and turns in the Communist Party's stance toward World War II.[32] They eventually supported the United States in the war and curtailed their activism. As a result, the Congress virtually ended as a political force. In this, they shared the fate of the rest of the Popular Front, according to Mario Garcia. "After 1941 other Popular Front organizations such as the American Youth Congress, the American Student Union, and the League of American Writers [who included Richard Wright as a member] existed only as paper organizations."[33]

Although the Congress died out as an organization, the activity of many of its members continued. Fierro de Bright was a leader in the defense of a group of young Chicano men wrongfully accused of murder in the "Sleepy Lagoon Case" of 1942.[34] Included on the ad hoc defense committee with Fierro was Carey McWilliams, who was among the first scholars to conduct a systematic study of Mexican immigrants and Mexican Americans. His writings coalesced in the 1949 book *North From Mexico,* whose ideas were the foundation for the Chicanos Studies movement. In concurring, Matt S. Meier wrote in the 1990 edition, "As the first, and until the beginning of the 1970s the only detailed general history of Mexicans in the United States, [*North From Mexico*] was destined to fill a unique niche in and have an enormous impact on the just-emerging field of Mexican American studies."[35]

McWilliams' collaboration with Josefina Fierro de Bright also illustrated the support given to Mexican-American radicals by white liberal intellectuals in California, support that Tejanos did not receive. Fierro and others therefore identified themselves as members of a national and international movement that cut across racial lines. Labor and radical movements were also the one arena that allowed women greater influence, mainly as activists but also as intellectuals. Chicanas were the contemporaries of women such as Caroline Decker, a young Anglo organizer in California who worked among agricultural workers and longshoremen.[36] Along with the receptivity of American radicals to women as independent voices, there was a Mexican tradition of feminine action in radical and labor causes. Female participation in the Mexican Revolution (particularly in its more radical phase) undermined the myths of Mexican women as passive. The anarchist Magons, male radicals of that conflict, played an important role in forming the political consciousness of both Josefina Fierro and Emma Tenayuca. Labor groups such as the Casa del Obrero Mundial (House of the World's Workers) familiarized Mexican women and men with labor organization and radical politics. Groups such as the IWW were the beneficiaries of this in the U.S.[37] Due to these factors, Mexican-American women were more active and visible in Popular Front groups in 1930s California than in LULAC.

Mexican Americans in Texas and California had many important conditions in common. They shared a racial heritage, culture, and language that was different from the surrounding Anglo-American environment. Both were the objects of discrimination, exclusion, and economic marginalization. However, the Tejano of San Antonio and the Chicano of Los Angeles lived in worlds that were different in subtle but crucial ways.

Mexican immigrants to South Texas arrived in a society that had living historical ties to its Mexican past. The surrounding white culture, composed of mostly southern Anglos, although often hostile shared many cultural attributes with Mexican society, such as a strong emotional attachment to the land, history, and family. In California, such historical ties were negligible, and immigrants found themselves there under an aggressive effort to acculturate them as Americans by Midwestern Americans whose individualistic values were totally foreign. Complicating this was the relative lack of intellectual leadership within the Mexican-American community.[38]

But more importantly, the creation of an American identity among Mexican immigrants was repeatedly hindered by ideological and physical assaults by Anglos, such as the repatriations in the Depression, the Sleepy

Lagoon trial, and the Zoot Suit Riots. All of these incidents received heavy coverage in the local media, nearly all of it depicting Mexicans as burdens on the public welfare, or as the conveyors of crime and disorder. This image, along with the Americanization programs of California progressives, left a psychological wound on the mind of immigrants and their children.

Excluded in California from mainstream politics, many Chicanos joined with other dispossessed Americans in the thirties under the Popular Front, the communist-led umbrella movement. While the aims of the Front were varied, many Mexicans were attracted to its emphasis on social and economic justice. They also believed themselves to be part of a phenomenon that cut across racial and even national barriers. In 1938 the Congress of Spanish-speaking Peoples became a major vehicle for the improvement of both Mexicans and Chicanos in California. Unlike Texas, the Congress found succor among a culture of radical Anglo intellectuals. This explained the effectiveness and influence of the Congress in California compared with Emma Tenayuca in San Antonio. The Congress and the rest of the Popular Front were also more open to women in active leadership. The careers of Josefina Fierro de Bright and Caroline Decker were examples of how women took leading roles in the California movement.

Two different visions of Mexican-American identity were developing in San Antonio and Los Angeles. In Texas, a mentality emerged that was male, politically moderate, middle-class, based on history, and integrationist. Mexican-American Californians continue to see themselves as Mexican, and members of an outsider class whose status in the area was provisional. Without a local history, many still looked to Mexico intellectually. Generally speaking, they were more accepting of radical ideologies and female authority. Such conditions were key in shaping the identity of California Chicanos, who assumed the intellectual leadership of Mexican Americans nationwide in the nineteen sixties, while Tejanos, who lived in a slightly different historical environment, made up much of its political leadership.

Chapter Five

Visions of Community, Part II

ARE WE GOOD NEIGHBORS? POST WAR MILITANCY

The service of thousands of Mexican Americans during World War II defined their identity throughout the nation and for the rest of the century. Veterans of that war would no longer accept discrimination against them. Increasingly they began to protest racial prejudice. Raul Morin, in his history of Mexican-American veterans of World War II and Korea, saw that "it did not matter whether we were looked upon as Mexicans, Mexican-American, [sic] or belonging to a minority group; the war soon made us all *genuine* Americans, eligible and available to fight and to defend our country."[1] During the war, the rhetoric of the Allies was filled with resounding affirmations of the equality of all races (including Mexican Americans) with Anglo Americans.

Risking their lives in the American cause removed all ambiguity Tejanos had about their place in the nation. "Mexican Americans [after the war] pushed by returning veterans and armed with the new identity of Mexican Americanism. . . did not ask 'Who am I?' they were now asking, 'What do we do?'"[2] Their joint participation with other Americans in a historical event of pivotal importance cemented their consciousness with the rest of America's ethnic groups.

Unlike other groups, however, Mexican-American culture and Mexican-American individuals were not accepted into U.S. culture and discourse. Brodkin noted that after World War II, elements of American Jewish culture were incorporated into the American marketplace of ideas, Jewish entertainers like Jack Benny were nationally acclaimed, and the New York Intellectuals became recognized commentators on the national scene.[3] In contrast, Richard Garcia observed that, "The Mexicans . . . were accepting American values, attitudes, and emotional responses, and they were expressing them through ideologies commensurate with their class position. But they were not accepted."[4]

Coupled with their new consciousness, racism against Tejanos continued during and after the Second World War, as the following postwar incidents

55

reveal: "Sargent [*sic*] Marcario Garcia of Sugarland, Texas, holder of the Congressional Medal of Honor, entered a restaurant in Richmond, Texas and asked for a cup of coffee. He protested when informed that the restaurant did not serve 'Mexicans.' An Anglo-American chased him out with a baseball bat." Across the state, conditions were no better: "Pat Tomas Garza was refused refreshments at the Ozuna Drug Store. He protested that his money was as good as anyone else's, whereupon the city sheriff, pistol in hand, ordered Pat Garza to leave the drug store."[5]

The product of these conditions (racial prejudice meeting a new identity) was that the actions and the rhetoric of Tejano thinkers and activists became less patient and more militant than earlier. Persons who had advocated a more gradual and conciliatory approach in the twenties and thirties had discarded this path in favor of demanding equal rights as a legitimate birthright. University of Texas professor and LULAC member Carlos Castañeda asserted, "Radical ailments require radical cures."[6] Although Tejanos still believed in working through the American system to acquire justice and equality, their demands on that system were more assertive. That assertiveness, in turn, grew out of their confidence as Americans and their refusal to tolerate the racial status quo.

Increasingly, Tejanos turned their energies from civic education and of cultural assimilation of their community to direct efforts to claim their rights as Americans. In the postwar era, LULAC and others focused less on civic education and more on direct political advocacy. Before the war LULAC had engaged primarily in an inward process of "Americanizing" Mexican immigrants. In the late forties, intellectuals and activists assumed that Tejanos were American and that the cause of their backwardness was Anglo oppression, not flaws in the Mexican character. Whites who maintained the racial and ethnic caste system in Texas were equated with the recently defeated German Nazis. Texas teacher J. Luz Saenz said as much: "We destroyed or are trying to destroy Hitler's racial theory. Why not the same thing with [Mississippi Senator Theodore] Bilbo and his imitators here in Texas, or in any other part of our Union?"[7]

The new attitude of Tejanos about white American society began to unite Mexican Americans with blacks and white liberals into a new political coalition. The main issue of this coalition was race relations. John Frederick Martin observed about the emerging movement that, "After 1945, and through the 1960's [*sic*] civil-rights would stand in the center of liberalism, the symbol of a new and vigorous creed."[8]

THE AMERICAN G.I. FORUM

The creation of the American G.I. Forum on March 26, 1948 in Corpus Christi, Texas was an early manifestation of this new identity. Dr. Hector Garcia, a dentist and World War II veteran founded the Forum due to the widespread discrimination against Mexican-American veterans, especially with regard to the recently passed G.I. Bill of Rights.[9]

Few laws have had the effect on American society that the G.I. Bill did. Over time, it would help transform the nation from a population of farmers and factory workers into middle-class college-educated professionals. Manuel Gonzales concurred in this assessment. "Signed into law by President Roosevelt on June 22, 1944, this path breaking act, one of the most powerful forces for social change in American history, paid for the education of 7.8 million soldiers re-entering civilian life, many of them Mexican veterans."[10]

Guaranteeing Mexican Americans complete and equal access to the benefits of the G.I. Bill was Garcia's primary objective. As time went on, the Forum became a leading advocate of Civil Rights in all areas. In 1954 it underwrote Gus Garcia in his handling of the *Hernandez* Supreme Court case. Because of the Forum's veteran constituency, it differed from LULAC and from other liberal organizations. Its members came from all classes of Tejano society, making the Forum more socially inclusive and more of a grass-roots organization. As Judy Lenninger Pycior discussed, "Unlike Lulacers, [Forum members] did not have to emphasize their knowledge of English and their professional status in order to prove their citizenship to skeptical Anglos. No matter how poor or dark-skinned, a veteran had the best possible U.S. pedigree."[11]

The Forum's makeup also made it impervious to attacks suffered by other liberal groups during the McCarthy years. Ignacio Garcia noted that loyalty of the Forum could not be questioned. "Mexican Americans had to demand their rights not only as citizens but also as veterans who have offered their lives to defend their country." As a result, this identity gave the Forum "Protection . . . against being labeled Communists or radicals."[12]

Their identity as Americans gave the Forum the confidence to become politically involved in a bolder and more explicit way than LULAC had. Historically, Americans normally begin political activity on the local level, addressing themselves to local issues. As the Progressives a century ago did, they often realized that local issues had causes that were national in scope. In the same way, the Forum discovered, in Henry Ramos words, "the need for substantially greater influence in the political arena."[13]

The Forum began to involve itself increasingly with the postwar liberal reform movement in its common goal of integrating American society. In addition, the unprecedented economic growth after 1945 allowed Tejanos to give their time and resources to the Forum and its causes. Though they still lagged behind the rest of the country, by the fifties "Mexican Americans were becoming, to some degree, more part of David Potter's 'People of Plenty'," according to Richard Garcia.[14] South Texas would produce the majority of the Mexican-American community's national leadership, convinced of their American identity by the war and supported organizationally by the grassroots structure created by the G.I. Forum.

ARE WE GOOD NEIGHBORS?

The writings of San Antonio attorney Alonso Perales and his fellow Tejano intellectuals mirrored the new realization occurring in the G.I. Forum. They believed that the Second World War, both in its rhetoric and its reality, had united Mexican immigrants and their children with the rest of the nation as no other event had (opposite to the experience of California Chicanos at the same time). After the sacrifice of so many Mexican Americans to purge the evils abroad, the renewed discrimination occurring after the war was unacceptable. Perales and many others felt it was time to remove domestic problems of racial injustice and hatred. In an important departure from their previous tactics, they placed the responsibility for injustice on the Anglo community, and looked to the federal government to rectify the situation.

The monograph *Are We Good Neighbors?* edited by Perales in 1948, embodied this new identity and approach to American society. The title sprang from the Good Neighbor policy of the Franklin D. Roosevelt administration, a diplomatic policy that professed a greater respect for the people and nations of Latin America. As Perales and other contributors of the book pointed out, respect and the equality were not given to Latin American citizens in the U.S., especially by white Texans. In congressional testimony contained in the book, Carlos Castañeda claimed that: "The Mexican American has been and is the victim of discrimination throughout the Southwest from Texas to California to such an extent that in many instances, and in many localities within this area, his condition is inferior to that of the Negro in the Deep South."[15]

Are We Good Neighbors? was a collection of articles, congressional and legal testimony outlining the condition of Mexican Americans in the Southwest. More importantly, it represented a united demand for civil rights and social equality by the Mexican-American generation to postwar United States. It was revealing and graphic in its content, confrontational in its tone. In keeping with the new militancy was a more explicit airing of discrimination and its effect on the community. Another contributor, J. Luz Saenz, blasted the substandard educational system provided Tejano children, saying that "A great number of our children never go beyond these segregated schools. Can you imagine what is the result? Those who never go beyond them either accept the pernicious notion of 'Inferiority Complex' or lose faith and trust in American ideals and the American people."[16] Elsewhere he writes, "Many of our boys in full uniform and bemedaled as heroes that they were, returning home on furlough . . . were thrown out of the BLUE MOON [caps in quote] dancing hall. We need not say a word of how some of their relatives were treated while they were fighting on behalf of democracy."[17]

The militant mentality of Saenz, Castañeda, and Hector Garcia contradicted an image of passivity and ineffectiveness created by Chicano-movement scholars in the seventies. Books like *Are We Good Neighbors?* and the activism of Garcia and the G.I. Forum reveal Tejanos angered by the climate of racial injustice around them after they had loyally defended their country. This anger took organized and articulate forms during the forties and fifties, and would lay a foundation for future movements.

Opportunities and obstacles became fuel for this new activism. Henry Ramos observed that "During the war, Mexican-American [sic] men and women were exposed to new possibilities in areas ranging from military-related service and travel to non-traditional employment."[18] Exposure to new opportunity, coupled with a new sense of identity, was a common phenomenon for many other immigrant groups in the U.S. Mexican Americans faced distinctive obstacles unique to their experience. The cause of these was racial and linguistic. Like African-Americans, Tejanos encountered discrimination throughout Texas. In California, they were confronted with a seemingly benign but pervasive educational system that tended to strip them of their cultural identity. Although limitations to the economic advancement of Mexican Americans were receding, they were still present, as David Bogue related in 1959: "The Mexican Americans constitute the only ethnic group for which a comparison of the characteristics of the first and second generation fails to show a substantial intergenerational rise in socio-economic status."[19]

SAN ANTONIO, 1945–1961: A TALE OF TWO CITIES

As San Antonio entered the postwar era, new opportunities emerged for it and its Mexican-American population, at the same time that the old problems of poverty still gripped the city. While many Tejano businessmen and professionals began to move into more prosperous sections of town (liberated from restrictive covenants by the Supreme Court) the West Side was still steeped in hopelessness. Also, the steady flow of immigration, both legal and illegal, continued from Mexico. Culturally and intellectually the newcomers replenished the Mexican mentality of the West Side. Although refugees from World War II did the same for the ethnic enclaves in the Midwest and Northeast, immigrants did not come to those areas on the scale that Mexicans entered the Southwestern U.S.

Immigration combined with the exodus of rural Tejanos to the cities made San Antonio the capital of Mexican-American life in Texas and one of the leading cities of the Southwest. By 1960, Rudolfo Acuña noted that "San Antonio . . . was unquestionably the most important Texas city for Chicanos in terms of both history and population. San Antonio had a Mexican population of 243,627, 17.2% of all the Mexicanos in the state."[20] Richard Garcia also believed that "The Alamo (which was the symbol of Texas independence from Mexico) made it, as far as Texas intellectual thought was concerned, the historical center of the state."[21]

National and international events combined to grow the city. Large defense budgets created by the Cold War deepened the involvement of the

Defense Department in San Antonio's economy. Also, the federal interstate highway system made San Antonio more accessible as a tourist destination and as a center of trade between the United States and Mexico. Global and national economic forces now had greater influence.

Simultaneously, San Antonio continued to struggle with problems of persistent and serious poverty, coupled with a wage market that was depressed relative to the rest of the country. An anti-union, southern mentality among the city's commercial elite prevented heavy industry from entering. Consistent with most southern cities, the economy rested on a low-wage base of agriculture, tourism and service industry, and the military. So while economic factors were pulling San Antonio into the present, there were equally strong forces attempting to maintain the status quo.

The city's economic structure was one of the many causes of the worst conditions of poverty in the nation concentrated on San Antonio's West Side, where the Mexican-American population predominated. Reverend Ralph Ruiz, a local Catholic priest, in testifying before the U.S. Commission On Civil Rights on December 1967, read a report that charged, "in this city 28 percent of the families make less than $3,000 per year, and over 6 percent of the families had an income of less than a thousand, although the economic picture appears optimistic and growth seems certain, it is still true that San Antonio has more area blight today than ever before." In the same testimony, Rev. Ruiz decried the fact that malnutrition was widespread in spite of welfare and food stamp programs.[22] Many observers commented that this poverty was concentrated on the Tejano West Side of the city, and strongly suspected that the reason for such conditions was rooted in residential segregation arising out of prejudice. Eugene Rodriguez noted along this line that, "Relatively segregated on the west side [sic] of town, most Latin Americans were wallowing in disease, poverty, filth, and illiteracy which was unparalleled in the worst slums of the East or the deep South [sic]. The nationally-noted correspondent Heywood Broun, called San Antonio's slums 'the worst in America.'"[23] It was on the stage of expanding promise, yet persistent and deep poverty, that Mexican-American politicians and intellectuals would perform their roles in the next 40 years.

HENRY B. GONZALEZ: AN AMERICAN OF MEXICAN DESCENT

At the University Of Colorado at Boulder on August 4, 1973, the elder statesman of Mexican-American congressmen, Henry B. Gonzalez of San Antonio (1916–2000) was scheduled to speak. Throughout the fifties and sixties, "Henry B." as he was known to his supporters, had been a pioneer in Texas politics and a tireless worker for civil rights at local, state, and national levels. As a soldier in the crusade for integration, his credentials were unequaled.

But during the late sixties and seventies, a new movement among Mexican Americans arose in communities from San Antonio to the West Coast, with a wide following in Colorado. The Chicano or Brown Power movement[24] was a product of varying generational and regional experiences among Mexican Americans throughout the nation. Like the Black Power movement (which it interacted with and borrowed from) Chicanismo emphasized cultural exceptionalism. Its ideology looked upon the American political, cultural, and economic system as inherently undemocratic, oppressive, and intent on destroying Mexican-American culture. By rejecting the values of America, Chicanos were often also rejecting the values of their parents, paralleling the counterculture movement among American youth in general.

For this reason, Chicano student activists at UC Boulder saw Gonzalez as a traitor to his race. When the Congressman arrived on campus for a series of meetings with students, according to him, they were nearly his last. In a 1980 interview with *Texas Observer* editor Ronnie Dugger, Gonzalez related the following: "About a dozen young people spirited him into a room at the University. Their leader . . . sat down and announced, 'You, Henry Gonzalez, are on trial. We demand that tonight you do not appear on the lecture platform unless you are prepared to denounce the Gringo Establishment and the mistreatment of Chicanos.'

Gonzalez thought he was kidding; 'What did you say your name was?' he asked.

'You don't talk tonight' said his judge, 'unless you talk about Chicano rights.' Gonzalez, still polite, said he could not honor that request. 'We're not requesting, we're demanding.' said the judge."

After heated rhetoric and profanity ensued, Gonzalez claimed that the students attempted to physically intimidate him. "A large youth came from his right flank, doubling a fist . . . all of them rose and moved toward him.

The judge proclaimed, 'we find you guilty and you are a traitor.' Gonzalez responded, 'Well, you're a little dumb s___.'" After more recriminations, the radicals threatened to be at the meeting that evening.

At the lecture hall, Gonzalez found demonstrators outside and his radical "jury" blocking the doors. Inside, the students ripped out the speaker's microphone and more menacingly, "Four of them had guns and seem to be hopped up on something." Using threat and subterfuge, Gonzalez was able to get himself, a professor, and his wife out of the building, but not before being spat upon and having chairs thrown at them.[25]

The violent protest against Gonzalez proved all too typical of the rhetorical, ideological, and at times even physical division breaking apart the Mexican-American Civil Rights movement, and left of center causes throughout the country generally. Dugger adroitly summed up the situation for Tejanos between 1968 and 1973: "Not the marching-together camaraderie of a vanguard minority, but the vitriolic divisions of charge and counter-charge, bite and bite back, physical walk-outs and emotional blowouts, fundamental disagreements about how to proceed politically, differences of status and purpose, and the blood-laden wake of the Vietnam

War left the mexicanos, [sic] as it left the whole American progressive movement, sad and exhausted."[26]

Enrique B. Gonzalez was born on May 3, 1916, five years after his family had fled to San Antonio from the town of Mapimi in Durango, Mexico, where his father was mayor of the city and was heir to the local silver mines. Gonzalez' ancestors had arrived there from Spain in 1561 and had owned the mines (operated by destitute Indian peons) and had controlled the city's politics.[27]

In 1911, this semi-feudal existence came to an end when Mexicans revolted against the dictatorship of Porfirio Diaz. The Gonzalez family became almost immediately a target of the Revolution, and Henry's father Leonides was almost executed by firing squad on two occasions.[28] Forced to leave Mexico, the family arrived in San Antonio almost penniless and became part of the Mexican community in exile.[29] Leonides Gonzalez became the general manager of *La Prensa,* the Spanish daily that was the intellectual voice of the exiles. Of all Leonides' children, Henry took most readily to his father's interest in the life of letters, reading in the newspaper's extensive library, and conversing with the exiles who met in the Gonzalez home for discussions on politics and other subjects.[30]

As a child, Henry Gonzalez felt the sting of racial prejudice, even from teachers in his elementary school.[31] His father told him, "We're Mexicans and we're here as sojourners," and his mother warned, "Oh, don't antagonize the Americans–this is their country."[32] An incident revealed the dual worlds Henry existed in. At school, he told his teacher that he was Mexican, but his instructor disagreed asserting that Henry's birth in San Antonio made him an American. According to Eugene Rodriguez, "this seemed logical to Gonzalez until he brought the matter up at home and 'Nana' [the housekeeper] ridiculed him by saying 'I guess if a cat is born in an oven, that makes him a loaf of bread.' This jolted his senses and carved a deep impression on his mind. The ambivalent atmosphere that the family was living in was rudely brought to his attention. Was he Mexican or American?"[33] From very early in life Henry B. Gonzalez was forced to confront issues of identity that nearly every first-generation American has had to address at one time or another.

After graduating from high school, Gonzalez enrolled with his older brother at the University of Texas, but Depression-era poverty and the generally hostile climate of Austin toward Tejanos forced him to leave there and enter St. Mary's Law School. Although he graduated, Gonzalez never completed the bar exam.

During World War II, Gonzalez took a position in the U.S. military intelligence, intercepting coded messages from Axis spies working in Mexico. In 1944, he was hired as a county juvenile probation officer. Two years later Gonzalez assumed the first of many pioneering positions by becoming the first Tejano chief probation officer in the history of Bexar County. Henry B. Gonzalez worked directly in the neighborhoods most affected by the crime and squalor of San Antonio. Throughout his career he would use this grass roots, populist approach, a tactic that made him one of the most popular figures in the region. In an interview, he said of those days "You work with the people, you live with them. You have to go to 'em."[34]

As time progressed, Gonzalez became more interested in political activity as a means of reforming conditions within the Tejano community. In 1950, he went to see Gus Garcia, recently elected to the San Antonio District School Board, to ask if Garcia would run for the state legislature. This was after Garcia had made an eloquent speech calling for Mexican-American involvement in the political process. However, the attorney begged off, claiming that "A Mexican couldn't win," and "It doesn't pay anything."[35] In the view of Eugene Rodriguez, these answers disturbed Gonzalez "who could not reconcile [Garcia's] public speeches demanding political action with . . . private statements of defeatism and selfishness."[36]

PARENTHETICAL: A PERCEPTION OF INFERIORITY

The apparent contradiction might be explained by a sense of inferiority many Mexican Americans were burdened with, especially Mexican-American men. It is crucial to point out, as did Samuel Ramos, "Not that the Mexican is inferior, but that he feels inferior."[37] Mexican intellectuals such as Ramos and Octavio Paz argued that such feelings of inferiority are a major feature of the Mexican character.

As discussed in Chapter One, Paz and Ramos held that this complex had its genesis in the encounter between the indigenous culture of Mexico, with its generally passive stance toward the environment, and the European culture that sought to shape and even conquer its surroundings. The resulting mestizo society was made to feel backward and forced to perpetually imitate European models. Like the Transcendentalists in the nineteenth century U.S., Ramos believed that by imitating the forms and philosophies of Europe, Mexico was inhibited from creating a culture that would be relevant to the nation's spiritual needs.[38] Paz agreed, explaining that "an inferiority complex influenced our preference for analysis, and that the meagerness of our creative output was due not so much to the growth of our critical faculties at the expense of our creativity, as to our instinctive doubts about our abilities."[39] Ironically, Van Wyk Brooks and other observers of mainstream U. S. culture used a nearly identical critique of imitation in the years around World War I.

Like African Americans, Mexican Americans were subjected to decades of discrimination and segregation that relegated them to the lower margins of American society. However, the exclusion suffered by Tejanos and Chicanos differed from the black experience in several important respects. Mexicans had already been the targets of exploitation for centuries at the hands of Spain, and by their wealthy Creole descendants after Mexican Independence.

The ambiguity of identity Mexicans suffered when they immigrated to the U.S. was compounded by discrimination. In addition to all the adjustments that a newcomer was forced to make, the Mexican was confronted with his or her internal contradictions in a society that saw them only as a source of cheap labor and the member of an inferior race.

Second, unlike blacks and other immigrants, there was no collective organization tied to Mexican culture to serve as a mediator or way station between the individual and U.S. culture. For European immigrants and blacks, the church acted as a miniature political environment apart from hostile surroundings, where leadership could be trained and the community could find solidarity. In contrast, George J. Sanchez noted that the organized Church was not a homegrown institution: "Unlike other largely Catholic immigrants to the United States, Mexicans did not bring significant numbers of migrating clergy with them."[40] The ambivalent relationship of Mexicans with the organized Catholic Church, dating from the colonial period (see Chapter One) could be responsible for this. He also found that "taken out of its community-based context in Mexico, religion appealed less to men."[41]

In addition, Mexican-American political organizations had to be created virtually from scratch, since generally they did not import political causes or practices from Mexico. Leonides Gonzalez, Henry's father, bore this out in an interview when he said, "I am grateful for the hospitality the United States has afforded . . . it has given me the protection of its laws. I will not immerse myself in its politics."[42] Therefore, no political tradition was imported into the U.S. that had a long-lasting impact for a majority of Mexican immigrants. This was in contrast to the Irish, who brought over political, linguistic, and religious practices that served them well in their adopted homeland.[43]

Consequently, Tejanos like Gus Garcia and Henry Gonzalez were thrown upon their own personal resources when they entered American politics. Unlike the case of Al Smith in Tammany Hall, they did not have a political system built into their cultural milieu where they could gain experience and confidence. As a result, many of their actions were tentative, self-limiting, and often self-defeating.

In 1950 Gonzalez ran unsuccessfully for state representative. Despite defeat, he inspired a large turnout of voters on the West Side that made victory possible for Maury Maverick, Jr. (son of the former liberal congressman), forging a lifelong alliance.[44] Gonzalez' long, painful rise to power began in 1953 when he was elected to the San Antonio City Council, and where he immediately became a thorn in the side of the city's Anglo elite.

When Henry B. Gonzalez ran for the State Senate in the Democratic primary, his colleagues on the Council paid for his filing fee, some out of support for him, others because they wanted to "kick him upstairs."[45] Racism still hung over the Texas consciousness like a cloud. Ronnie Dugger observed, "The prejudice had virulence and currency that are almost inconceivable to younger people now."[46] After Gonzalez defeated his Democratic opponent, Ozzie Latimer, he became the only Democrat in Bexar County contested in the general election by a Republican, who admitted that he would not have opposed Latimer.[47] Gonzalez overcame this racially-motivated opposition to become the first Tejano elected to the Texas Senate in the twentieth century.

It was as a member of the Texas Senate that Henry B. Gonzalez made his entrance onto the national and state political stage. Because he could not afford the cost of a hotel room or apartment in Austin, Gonzalez had to commute 80 miles during the legislature's biennial or special sessions. Yet even that obstacle did not prevent him from making Texas legislative history.

Ten bills designed to circumvent or defy *Brown v. Board Of Education* were proposed during the 1957 session.[48] Along with three other South Texas senators, Gonzalez held the floor for 36 hours in an attempt to kill the proposals by filibuster. More than one publication noticed the irony of the use of a legislative tactic traditionally used to protect Jim Crow, now directed against it.[49]

During his twenty-two hour stint on the floor of the Texas Senate, Gonzalez drew on his experience as the member of a segregated minority. Although the bills in question were directed against the integration of blacks, Gonzalez warned that they would create a hostile climate to him and other Mexican Americans. An article in *Time* magazine related how Gonzalez "told of being barred from a cafe table because he was a Mexican"[50] and how he could not go to park in the primarily German-American town of New Braunfels for the same reason.[51]

The senator also relied on a personal store of knowledge acquired from a lifetime of study. In so doing, he linked the struggle of the African American and the Mexican American with the struggle for freedom throughout the entire history of the West. Elaborating, Gonzalez said, "The Irish have a saying, 'it is easy to sleep on another man's wounds . . . well, what's the difference? Mexican, Negro, what have you. The assault on the inward dignity of man, which our sovereignty protects, has been made. We all know in our hearts and in our minds that it is wrong.'"[52]

Eugene Rodriguez also noted that Gonzalez combined his minority status with his understanding of the American and Western literary traditions for the purpose of integrating minorities intellectually, politically, and socially. Rodriguez wrote, "The many years of constant pursuit of all the teachings and writings of the scholars of the Western World, coupled with his own experiences as the member of a minority ethnic group enabled Gonzalez to fluidly and intelligently tell the people of Texas of the evils of segregation and the folly of the ten segregation bills introduced in the Legislature."[53] He also concluded that without Gonzalez's vigorous and articulate advocacy, "Texas could well have reverted to the degenerate atmosphere on human relations that [plagued] Mississippi and Alabama."[54]

As a result of the talkathon, Gonzalez, Sen. Abraham Kazen (a second-generation Lebanese American) and other legislators defeated all but two of the segregation proposals. Gonzalez was catapulted into national stature within the Democratic Party and the civil rights movement. In 1960 he was named vice-chairman of the national Viva Kennedy Clubs, a group of Mexican Americans supporting the election of John F. Kennedy to the presidency. (Some have argued that Viva Kennedy's independence from the Democratic Party marked the beginning of the political nationalism of the Chicano movement. Many young organizers in Viva Kennedy would be influential later in the decade.)

After unsuccessful runs for governor and U.S. Senator, Henry B. Gonzalez was elected to the twentieth Congressional District in a special election in 1961, becoming the elder statesman of Mexican-American politicians and, at that time, the highest-ranking Tejano in the government. Being in a critical place on the national stage as a representative of Mexican Americans nationwide, Gonzalez would often speak on questions of Mexican-American identity. It would be these very questions where he would face new and difficult challenges.

GONZALEZ AND THE CHICANO MOVEMENT

On April 10, 1969 the 24-year-old founder of the Mexican American Youth Organization (MAYO), Jose Angel Gutierrez, held a news conference at MAYO headquarters on the West Side of San Antonio. In a prepared statement, he announced that "MAYO has found that federal and religious programs aimed at social change do not meet the needs of Mexicanos in the state."

"Further," he reported "we find that the vicious cultural genocide being inflicted upon La Raza by gringos and their institutions not only severely damage our human dignity, but also make it impossible for La Raza to develop its right of self-determination."[55] As he continued, Gutierrez articulated his purpose more clearly: "Our organization, largely composed of youth," he said, "is committed to effecting meaningful social change. Social change that will enable La Raza to become masters of their destiny, owners of their resources . . . as a culturally and spiritually distinct people from the gringo." In conclusion, Gutierrez summarized the relations of MAYO with the Anglos and other Mexicans. "MAYO will not engage in controversy with fellow Mexicanos," he promised, "regardless of how unfounded and vindictive their actions may be. We realize the effects of cultural genocide will take many forms — some Mexicanos will become psychologically castrated . . . others will come together, resist and eliminate the gringo. We will be with the latter."

Although Gutierrez maintained that using the phrase "eliminate the gringo" metaphorically, he left open the possibility of violence "If nothing else will work." His words frightened and agitated the audience of mostly

Anglo media, one of whom introduced his article on Gutierrez by asserting that "gringo-dominated society is responsible for the problems of the Mexican-American 'barrios' and unless there is social change there is a possibility of violence and rioting as a result of 'very serious social unrest.'"[56] For San Antonio, a city that had mostly escaped the national upheaval of the previous two years, it was a disturbing prospect. For Gutierrez, the statement known as the "kill the gringo" speech became a defining moment in his career as an activist, one which he would later try to back away from.[57]

JOSE ANGEL GUTIERREZ

Jose Angel Gutierrez (1944–) was born in Crystal City in the "Winter Garden" region of South Texas, where Mexicans formed 85% of the population, but who had virtually no power. Coming from a middle-class family, Gutierrez obtained a B.A. in political science from Texas A&M University at Kingsville, and was a graduate student at St. Mary's University in the summer of 1967 when he founded MAYO along with four other activists. Political scientist Antonio Navarro asserted that MAYO was different from other protest movements of the period in that its organization was carefully planned and thought out, not spontaneous.[58] Three important contemporary movements influenced them: the New Left, the African American Civil Rights movement, and the emerging Chicano movement.

As the five founders of MAYO discussed issues and problems facing Mexican Americans, they also examined the changing political and intellectual climate around them. During the Vietnam War period, college students became a new force of activism in the nation. According to Juan Patlan, another of the founders of MAYO, "Some of the ideas of the New Left were also topics of discussion" during the group's early meetings.[59] Julie Lenninger Pycior, another student of the period, made this important observation about MAYO's connections: "Gutierrez and UMAS leaders were following a path blazed several years earlier by Chicanas active in SNCC [Student Non-violent Coordinating Committee] and the radical student movement. María Varela (a Mexican American from Milwaukee) organized disenfranchised black residents in the Deep South for SNCC."[60]

More important were movements for social justice carried out by black Americans, both the nonviolent, integrationist efforts of Dr. Martin Luther King, Jr. and the more violent, nationalistic Black Power movement. Its ties to MAYO were direct, as Gutierrez and other leaders "Traveled . . . into the southern part of the United States to talk to [Stokley] Carmichael and the organizers of [King's] Southern Christian Leadership Conference."[61] Elsewhere, Navarro observed that "The civil-rights and Black Power movements significantly affected the thinking of [MAYO's founders]."[62] At one point in a heated speech, Gutierrez declared, "our devil has pale skin and blue eyes,"[63] in language strongly reminiscent of Malcolm X. In rhetoric, strategy, and ideology, MAYO borrowed from black struggles for equality and respect. According to Manuel Gonzales, "What made the difference was the changing intellectual climate in America, especially the rise of the black civil-rights movement."[64] Other racial minorities, especially in the younger generation, now felt free to question the racial justice of American society.

The Chicano movement was the main ideological and motivational force behind MAYO and its affiliated groups. The word "Chicano" is of imprecise origin. Richard Garcia discovered that during the early part of the last century a "very popular song among the poor (who often called themselves Chicanos) was the corrido entitled 'El Chicano,' which captured their thinking about going north from Mexico. One of the verses dealt with the almost inevitable theme of acculturation."[65] Whatever its beginning, the word Chicano had strong connotations of self-identity. Gutierrez noted that "Back in the early fifties a lot of Mexicanos who are different in terms of their lifestyles, in terms of their language, in terms of their aspirations were called *pachuco*. And now this same idea is applying to [Chicanos] those different Mexicans who are very militant, who are very aggressive in pursuit of what they deemed to be their self-interest."[66]

Both the Chicano and the *pachuco* [a term usually identified with gang members, the urban home-boy, the school dropout, and the delinquent] lived their lives in ways that were different from the American mainstream, and often in rebellion to it. The beatniks of the fifties lived in a similar fashion, although the Beat movement was more self-conscious than the *pachuco*.

This component of rebellion was one of the reasons for the opposition of most middle-class Tejanos in San Antonio, especially those of Henry B. Gonzalez's generation, to Chicanos like Gutierrez. The more conservative climate of the Mexican-American community there (living in the South and being imbued with the values of LULAC and the military during World War II and the Cold War) put the activists on the ideological fringes. To the Mexican-American generation, the pachuco and Chicano represented lawlessness, lack of initiative and a rejection of the corresponding American values of hard work and individual ambition that the older group felt were the key to their success. While Chicanos often found opposition in San Antonio, the same would not be true elsewhere.

THE RADICAL MOVEMENT

For a Mexican-American reporter in Los Angeles, "A Chicano is a Mexican American with a non-Anglo image of himself."[67] In Southern California, New Mexico, and even Colorado, Chicano militancy with its critique of Anglo-American society and its nationalistic outlook had a far more receptive audience than in San Antonio. For reasons discussed in the previous chapter, California's economy and political environment make it more open to radical causes. This was especially the case in the sixties, where many Anglo radicals who were the blood children of the Old Left took part in demonstrations such as the Free Speech riots at the University of California at Berkeley. The Bay Area was also home to the Black Panther Party, another important nationalist movement.

The California Chicano movement's most visible connection to the New Left was the Chicano Moratorium on August 29, 1970 in Los Angeles, where some 25,000 Chicanos protested American involvement in the Vietnam conflict, and the disproportionate number of casualties among Mexican Americans. The Chicano Moratorium, though independently organized, was patterned after the National Moratorium that occurred on October 15, 1969, according to Gutierrez.[68]

The cornerstone of Chicano ideology was cultural nationalism, the belief that Chicanos constituted a separate and distinct nation apart from a racially oppressive U.S.A newspaper of the Los Angeles Chicano student movement voiced this opinion. "Refusing to accept an imposed anglo [sic] value system," the article notes, "Chicanos are creating their own life style [sic] under the banner of cultural nationalism. A rich past of aztec [sic] and revolutionary heroes destroys the 'dirty Mexican' and 'lazy Mexican' labels. In other words, a positive self-image replaces a negative stereotype." Explaining, the writer says that "Nothing is told about the Indian and mexican [sic] side of history, nothing about the cruel and imperialistic anglo [sic] takeover." To remedy this injustice, Chicanos in California would attempt to reconnect themselves with their history, and to construct a new history. "By throwing out most of the garbage and lies that have been perpetrated on us, we construct another set of values that are more relevant to our needs. We teach our children about Joaquin Murietta, not Robin Hood, about Zapate, not Kit Carson. We rewrite the history of the Southwest."[69]

The intellectual currents running within the Chicano movement in California and elsewhere included a rejection of the American historical narrative in favor of a Mexican narrative. The new narrative and the values it contained were most compellingly articulated in Colorado by a major figure of the Chicano movement, Rudolfo "Corky" Gonzales (1928–). Born and raised in the barrios of Denver, Gonzales became a professional boxer in the 1950s to escape a life of poverty. By 1960, Gonzales was the Colorado coordinator of the Viva Kennedy campaign, and during the Johnson administration became Chairman of the Board in the local War on Poverty program.[70]

It was the War on Poverty that allowed Gonzales to become the voice of Chicano nationalism and caused him to reject the integrationist agenda of Lyndon Johnson and other liberals. Julie Lenninger Pycior commented on this: "The growing participation of barrio leaders in federal programs and national politics accelerated their integration into American life. Paradoxically, however, the successful lobbying efforts of the G.I. Forum, and LULAC . . . and others also reinforced a separate minority identity that would culminate in the anti-establishment Chicano movement."[71] Her assertion was born out when Gonzales resigned from the War on Poverty when he was accused of discriminating against poor Anglos and blacks.[72] Claiming that he was being co-opted and exploited by the Anglo political structure, Corky Gonzales formed the Crusade for Justice, a locally run community empowerment organization that promoted education, health services and community action. Gonzales believed that Mexican Americans ought to develop their own paths for personal and community reform, based on their values and language, separate from American society. The Crusade's organization and agenda reflected this, in that it returned to the politics of personalism espoused by James Tafolla, Sr. in the days before LULAC (see Chapter Two). Navarro took note of this by stating that "Gonzales and the Crusade were one. In the Crusade for Justice, as in many other movements, the leader *was* the organization [emphasis in text]. The presence of *personalismo*—the power of the charismatic personality–guided the formation and development of the Crusade. This meant that the Crusade's ideology . . . [was an] extension of its leadership–*el Jefe* Corky.[73]

Gonzales, Gutierrez, and other leaders of the Chicano movement were reflections of a new trend in the civil rights movement as a whole–a move toward groups that were opposed to assimilation with white America, led by personalities outside the political structure who were usually young, more culturally assertive, and more confrontational in their tactics, employing violent rhetoric, if not violence itself. This also implied a view of earlier groups and leaders as ineffective at best or at worst as traitors to their race. The youth also sensed that the white establishment chose the earlier generation, i.e., Martin Luther King, LULAC, and others, whereas the youth emerged directly from the community. Chicano leadership mirrored the same direction in politics and civil rights that occurred with figures such as Muhammad Ali within the culture of American sports.

Navarro also was aware of this trend. He said that "By 1967 Chicano youth became increasingly critical of what some scholars have called the 'Mexican American generation.' the discontent was predicated in part on the youth's utter rejection of the Mexican American generation's adherence to a more traditional, moderate, and work within the system approach. The epithets of vendidos (sellouts), and 'coconuts' (brown on the outside, white on the inside) became popular and commonplace in the vocabulary of Chicano youth leaders."[74] Although direct hostility by the Chicano activists toward the older generation, was muted[75] (in contrast with the New Left) there was an implicit rebuff of the integrationist American values held by the middle class and a desire to replace it with a set of values rooted in the Mexican experience.

Perhaps the best intellectual statement of the Chicano movement was penned by Corky Gonzales in 1967, entitled *I am Joaquín*. In this poem, the author identified himself with Joaquín Murrieta, a shadowy figure in 1850s California who allegedly carried out depredations against Anglos in retaliation for their taking land from Mexican settlers. In many ways the counterpart of Nat Turner, Joaquín was never arrested, nor was his exact identity ever known.[76]

I Am Joaquín eloquently recited the deeds and heroes of Mexican and Mexican-American history, but contrasted that history with the alienated status of the Chicano in modern American society. Like Allen Ginsberg in *Howl* and James Baldwin in his works, Gonzales finds the modern American environment spiritually wanting. They and other social critics saw the culture as a heartless machine that stamped out cookie-cutter Americans, while in the process crushing their souls. It is important to note however, that the prosperity and freedom of postwar America was the very thing that gave them the ability to make these critiques.

For the Mexican American, this crushing constituted the loss of language, culture and history. *I am Joaquín* was to inspire Chicanos to a new era of cultural nationalism and activism, but it was also designed to refute the argument that they were an ahistorical people. For Mexican Americans, pride in their history and culture would give them pride in themselves. The poem itself quickly became an anthem of the Chicano movement and was "Performed by theatre groups, young Chicanos at speech meets, beauty contests, and dramatic readings; and cited in speeches and essays by various Chicano leaders."[77]

THE IMAGE OF ATZLÁN

What distinguished Chicanos like Gonzales and Gutierrez from other radical protest movements of their time was the coalescence of their aspirations, either literally or metaphorically, into a geographical location–the territory of Aztlán. Aztlán was a location "in the far north" from where the ancient Aztecs were to have originated. While the story of Aztlán is legendary, it was historically appropriated by Chicano activists as the territory of the Southwest U.S. Manuel Gonzales observed that, "Rudolfo (Corky) Gonzales became the foremost champion of the idea that Aztlán, the mythical homeland of the Mexica, was to be found in the Southwest, which he and others called 'occupied America.' [He] called for the restoration of the ancestral land to the Chicanos."[78]

In describing the necessity for Aztlán, Ignacio Garcia explained how the legend identified past injustices and served to inspire Chicanos amid the difficulties of the present. "Chicanos [Corky Gonzales] insisted, had a psychological attachment to their land, and the Anglo Americans had stripped them of it to induce a cultural self-destruction that the barrios were facing. This land was the land of their ancestors, and those who crossed the river came not as strangers, but as sons and daughters of former Aztecs, seeking to claim what was once theirs. Gonzales knew that the concept of Aztlán went beyond a political or even the historical. It was mythical in proportions, and it had to be, to give Chicanos the collective strength to overcome the obstacles of poverty, assimilation, violence, and self-doubt they faced daily."[79]

Here was a total reinvention of identity. It aimed to ground the Mexican American in his or her historical roots, but in a history that was pre-Christian and non-European. Although the majority of Mexicans had arrived in the U.S. after 1910, and had never owned land there, many had come as landless peons, deprived of their communal lands in Mexico by the Diaz regime. The language of dispossession thus struck a deep chord in their psyche.

Aztlán was also a term of redemption, an attempt to recapture an Edenic state lost by conquest and racial oppression. It was also designed to introduce the Mexican American living in the middle of the twentieth century to their true nature. However, it is important to note that although the ideology surrounding Aztlán was the attempted reconstruction of a Mexican consciousness, it was a reconstruction within an American context. Just as black nationalists and the Nation of Islam interpreted their African heritage through the prism of their experience in white America, and could not become Africans, so the Mexican experience was articulated by Chicanos as citizens of United States.

Aztlán as a vehicle for Chicano cultural nationalism is also intriguing given that the option of pan-Mexicanism was never considered. Although their homeland was adjacent to the U.S., Chicanos like Gonzales and Gutierrez never considered reunification with Mexico a possibility. One might speculate that a pan-Mexican position (such as that assumed by the Mexican immigrant generation) would have created a host of difficulties regarding Mexican politics, identity, and the relationship between Mexico and Chicanos. Finally, the activists would also have had to confront the inevitable reality of Spanish ancestry. Instead, activists preferred to wage their battles in a familiar environment of the U.S. and emphasize the indigenous aspects of their identity. The dialectic of Aztlán served this purpose.

The ideals of cultural nationalism were further developed through a document called El Plan Espiritual de Aztlán (The Spiritual Plan of Aztlán). This document was the product of the Chicano National Youth Liberation Conference, held under the auspices of Gonzales' Crusade for Justice in Denver on March 1969. Calling for a renewal of Mexican consciousness based on an indigenous heritage, an embrace of a rural, communal existence, and a rejection of contemporary American values, cultural nationalism was the centerpiece of this manifesto, which ironically echoed the Declaration of Independence:

"Brotherhood unites us, and love for our brothers makes us a people whose time has come and who struggles [sic] against the foreigner 'gabacho' who exploits our riches and destroys our culture. With our heart in our hands and our hands in the soil, we declare the independence of our mestizo nation. We are a bronze people with a bronze culture. Before the world, before all of North America, before all our brothers in the bronze continent, we are a nation, we are union of free pueblos, we are Aztlán."

To make this vision a reality, the plan declared, "We can only conclude that social, economic, cultural and political independence is the only road to total liberation from oppression, exploitation, and racism."[80]

The Plan was a call for a redefinition of identity founded on a Mexican and indigenous consciousness, not an American one. Genero Padilla observed that this cultural nationalism during the 1960's was not unique. "Imamu Baraka, Ron Karenya, Carolyn Gerald, to name only a few Black writers and cultural theorists, were among those bent on reconstructing Black consciousness by challenging white cultural hegemonies and replacing them with neo-African symbols of blackness."[81]

Gutierrez and MAYO adopted the concept of cultural nationalism as their own, forming the La Raza Unida Party (RUP) in 1970 and rejecting the two-party system. RUP scored a number of important electoral successes in Gutierrez's Winter Garden region. In an interview, Gutierrez stated his belief that the electoral takeover of the local school board would allow Tejanos to advance educationally and avert possible violence. "The Chicanos here have completely taken over the school system." He declared, "This is where we can hurt the gringo most — in education. As long as we were illiterate slobs, we didn't stand a chance. But when we're educated, lawyers and doctors, well, we won't take nothing from nobody!"[82]

The impact of RUP in San Antonio, however, was not nearly as great. The reasons for this were fourfold. First, the ahistorical dialectic of Aztlan did not have the same appeal in a city with its own historical narrative. Many Tejanos did not feel they had to construct their own story, separate from the American story, in the way that Chicanos in California and Denver did. In this sense, Tejanos in San Antonio were tied to history, while the Chicano movement was less so.

Second, the mystic call back to the land contained in El Plan de Aztlan also was not an attractive option to San Antonians whose fortunes and culture were linked to a growing, increasingly modern city. This conceptual gap grew as the 1970s progressed, as Chabran and Fregoso astutely noted. "The shortsightedness of Chicanos Studies intellectuals," they pointed out, "was that they assumed that the construction of their own self representation . . . was equivalent to that of the totality of the Chicano experience, and that shared representation could be generalized in the interest of the entire group. How else could we explain . . . that an ahistorical 'Aztec' identity would fall on the deaf ears of an urban community versed in the rhythms of disco, conjunto music, and boleros?"[83] So while cultural nationalism as a political entity held the interest of the population in rural areas where Mexican Americans lived in apartheid-like situations or in cities with little or no historical consciousness such as Los Angeles, its strength in San Antonio was not great.

Still another feature of the Chicano movement that made it influential in California was the emergence of the Chicano Studies movement in the universities of that state, leading to what Thomas Bender has referred to as

"The professionalization of the intellect."[84] That is, the concentration of the life of the mind primarily within the academic disciplines, often to the exclusion of people in other walks of life. By 1970 this trend was occurring among minorities in the same way that it had affected the rest of the population earlier. A number of trends and events were responsible for this.

Due to the expansion of its population and economy, USC and the University of California system were among the fastest growing colleges in the country. The GI Bill also exponentially increased access to education nationwide. By 1970, Chicano students and many of their professors, propelled by the ideology of the Movement, created Chicano Studies departments that defined the Mexican-American experience across disciplines, and attracted talented students from across the nation, including Texas. With these resources at their command, California Chicanos became the most articulate arbiters of Mexican-American identity.

Finally, as Tejanos shifted their energies to politics, a change occurred on the Mexican-American landscape, with California producing cultural and ideological leadership, and Texas producing most of its political leadership. Pycior also noticed this inclination. "The two most important organizations of the Mexican American generation," she wrote, "LULAC and the GI Forum, originated in Texas, but most Chicano groups began in California, reflecting the fact that Los Angeles—with its two million Mexican-heritage residents, many of them young—had eclipsed San Antonio as the center of Mexican heritage life."[85]

The first organized meeting of the Chicano movement in San Antonio reflected this trend. Held on January 6, 1968 at John F. Kennedy High School on the West Side, "La Raza Unida" (not to be confused with the political party, formed a year later) featured as its keynote speaker Dr. Ernesto Galarza from San Jose California, a prominent author and consultant to the Ford Foundation.[86] Recipient of a doctorate from Columbia University, Galarza was representative of the new type of Mexican-American intellectual whose scholarship and activism were driven by the same ideology. Although he was a contemporary of Carlos Castañeda, Galarza would become a role model for younger Chicano scholars such as Rudolfo Acuña.

Even though Tejano groups such as MAYO and even the G.I. Forum were heavily represented at the gathering,[87] much of the conference's leadership was made up of Californians, such as Galarza and activist Bert Corona, who began his career with the Congress of Spanish-Speaking Peoples. The conference held workshops dealing with the condition of Mexican Americans. Significantly, virtually all of the gatherings were chaired by Californians, none from Texas or San Antonio. This was typical of the Chicano movement throughout its history.[88] Although they played an active role in the Texas political scene, Chicano thinkers operated primarily in California where intellectual resources were greater and the climate was more conducive to radical groups. Unfortunately, San Antonio would suffer a "brain drain."

The final obstacle faced by Chicano activists in introducing San Antonio Tejanos to a nationalist consciousness was the determined opposition of Henry B. Gonzalez. Although the battles between the congressman and Chicanos took place on a number of different levels, the focus here will be on the Mexican-American pluralistic vision that Gonzalez continued to articulate. In the process, he raised issues of identity facing every Mexican American.

Gonzalez began wrestling with such questions in an article he wrote for the national magazine of the AFL-CIO (organized labor was one of his consistent supporters) in 1967. Before discussing the social condition of Mexican Americans, Gonzalez remarked that "There is not even a generally accepted name for this minority group. Americans of Spanish surname are called Mexicans, Mexicanos, Latins, Latinos, Latin Americans and Hispanic Americans; not one of these labels is accepted everywhere. A name accepted in one place is enough to produce violence elsewhere."

Knowing this confusion of labels, Gonzalez proposed a name of his own. "I prefer to think of the group as Americans of Spanish surname because, after all, they are Americans and they all have Spanish surnames. Any other label would be inadequate because . . . [his] is not a single origin. He has come from different places, at different times and for different reasons. He is different from other immigrant groups in that his homeland, his mother country is not across the sea."[89]

The decision facing the Mexican Americans was whether individual Mexican Americans would assimilate into the larger culture, or retain their linguistic and cultural otherness by staying within their ethnic enclaves and risking individual success. He elaborated, "the Spanish-surnamed American is attempting to find a *modus vivendi* — a way to live somewhere between the intolerable extremes."[90]

In describing the difficult position encountered by Tejanos, Gonzalez agreed with social scientist Eric Hoffer that communities that refuse to assimilate often provide their members with a psychologically safe haven, while standing outside of the mainstream. In contrast, where outside values are encouraged and accepted the individual can be left on his or her own. According to the congressman, "If [a Tejano] elects to compete with the majority on its own terms then he must abandon [the safety of the community, and] then he becomes an outsider both to his own group and to the majority. He has abandoned the one and is seeking to invade the other."[91] The result of such outsider status, according to Hoffer, is that the minority member "is also burdened with a sense of guilt, however vague, of a renegade."[92]

Gonzalez's solution to this dilemma was a call to the larger society that it must provide room for other cultures, which would result in all feeling equally accepted. Gonzalez's pluralistic vision agreed with the multi-cultural paradigm articulated by Goizueta and Matovina, which asserted that "genuine pluralism entails the recognition that various groups or perspectives can coexist without dominating the others."[93] Along the same line,

Gonzalez asserted that, "Culture is too precious a thing to destroy; it must be permitted to make its own contributions to society, especially one like ours."[94] He was firmly committed to the vision of a nation that admitted minorities into its cultural, economic, and political mainstream while at the same time permitting them to maintain their cultural distinctiveness. In other words, he believed that community identity should not be threatened by individual advancement.

Consequently, Gonzalez perceived the cultural nationalism of Chicanos as a direct threat to this pluralistic vision. In fact, he likened them to the white segregationists he had filibustered against in 1957. In a speech before the U.S. House of Representatives meant as a reply to Gutierrez's remarks three months earlier, Gonzalez said that "I cannot accept the belief that racism in reverse is the answer for racism and discrimination; I cannot accept the belief that simple, blind, and stupid hatred is an adequate response to simple, blind and stupid hatred." Continuing, he vowed, "I have stood against racists before, and will do it again."[95]

Earlier in the same speech, Gonzalez introduced his audience to the struggles encountered by Tejanos interfacing with modern America, using many examples from his own life. It was one of the most effective discussions of minority identity. He said, "the individual [Mexican American] finds himself in conflict, sometimes with himself, sometimes with his family, sometimes with his whole world. What is he to be? Mexican? American? Both? How can he choose? Should he have pride and joy in his heritage, or bear it as a shame and sorrow? Should he live in one world or another, or attempt to bridge them both?" Gonzalez continued to describe the dilemmas of individual Tejanos and their stance toward the opportunities and perils represented in the American dream. "You never know whether you will be accepted or rejected in the larger world or whether your old friends will despise you for making the wrong choice. For a member of this minority, like any other, life begins with making hard choices about personal identity."[96]

The San Antonio Congressman hit upon the central difficulty confronting minorities, in fact, facing all Americans in modern U.S. society. As Americans seek material and professional success, the individualizing forces that encourage personal liberation and independence–an egalitarian college system, ease of travel, and the dominance of a mass consumer economy–tended to pull individuals away from their community roots and forced them to stand alone. While some Americans with an Emersonian bent found this empowering, it was often jarring to African Americans, Mexican Americans, and others who have relied upon their community for individual self-esteem. Gonzalez tried to solve this problem by making American society more pluralistic. Chicanos like Gutierrez attempted to opt out of American culture by creating a collective Chicano political and ideological consciousness. Later, he would lament that American society "is willing to allow individual upward mobility, but it will never allow a collective rise of our people."[97] Both Henry B. Gonzalez and Jose Angel Gutierrez desired to preserve a Mexican-American community in Texas and the United States. But as to the identity of that community (one accepting European cultural traditions, the other being skeptical of them) and the place of that community in the American political landscape, they were at loggerheads.

CHICANO ART IN SAN ANTONIO

Although Chicano ideology had little impact on San Antonio politically, its most lasting contribution was in the area of culture, specifically in the visual arts. Many young Tejanos were searching for an outlet to express questions arising out of what many saw as their "in-between" status. San Antonio artist David Gonzales remembered how the schools he attended discouraged his friends and him from speaking Spanish, and prevented them, in many cases, from acquiring knowledge of their Mexican past.[98] However, their family spoke Spanish and orally passed down their history at home. Young Tejano men and women had to deal with the twin realities of a Mexican past and a Mexican-American present. Their mechanism for accomplishing this was the medium of art, first working individually and informally, later by developing communities of artists who were asking the same questions and struggling with the same issues.

Chicano art is as eclectic and diverse as their history, making use of genres of graffiti, pre-Columbian indigenous art, Mexican religious symbols, and every type of American painting, photography, and sculpture. The themes featured the ideals of Chicano nationalism, Mexican history and heroes, and most importantly, scenes from everyday life. Like the African-American artists of the Harlem Renaissance, communities of artists in San Antonio like Con Safo used their talents to explore their community, their culture, their families, and themselves. Their ultimate object was to stimulate pride in being Mexican American and to serve as role models for the young. The achievements of Kathy Vargas, whose paintings have been recognized nationally, have demonstrated the potential contribution of Mexican Americans to the nation's artistic life.

In some ways, Chicano artists became the victims of their own success. The early ideological motivation for many of them was the cultural mandate in El Plan de Atlán: "We must insure that our writers, poets, musicians, and artists produce literature and art that is appealing to our people and relates to our revolutionary culture."[99] When their art was shown in major galleries in New York, the nationalistic underpinnings of their work appeared to be undermined, causing no little degree of angst. Richard Hofstadter observed that even revolutionary art can be included in the "grab-bag" of American culture, and that has been a source of constant disappointment to revolutionaries of all types. "The frustration of the modern intellectual lies in the co-optive powers of American society," observed Hofstadter. "Yesterday's revolution is today's fad. Everything is bought off, absorbed, drawn to the center."[100]

It was through the arts that the ideal of a bronze nation contained in Chicano nationalism had its most lasting affects. As La Raza Unida and other political manifestations of Brown Power began to fade with other social movements in the 1970s, the cultural pride promoted by Corky Gonzales and others continued. A history of one of the most important voices of the movement, the journal *El Grito*, bears this out. Begun in 1967 in Southern California by Chicano activist Octavio Romano, *El Grito* was a vehicle of Chicano thought on nearly every related subject. Its overall purpose, according to Richard Garcia, was to call "for a redeeming of the historical and collective consciousness of lo mexicano."[101] Like Corky Gonzales, Romano sought to base Chicano identity on a Mexican foundation. The early editions of *El Grito* attempted to accomplish this through the inclusion of documents, news and research articles, fiction, poetry and art. In many ways it mirrored the earlier efforts of Perales in *Are We Good Neighbors?* by attempting to create a new mindset among its readers.

By the closing edition in 1973, *El Grito* was devoted almost exclusively to literature and art, indicating a possible frustration of the editors with political activity and ideological polemic. While the move away from activism and into culture may be interpreted as a retreat, it could also be seen as an adjustment by the activists for the hearts and minds of the Mexican-American community. Art can be used to speak to the consciousness far more powerfully than prose or political activism. Novels such as *Uncle Tom's Cabin* and the poems of Walt Whitman give evidence of this.

Two Visions of Identity

With the end of the Second World War, the development of Mexican-American identity entered a new stage. The service of thousands in the Armed Forces gave the minority the conviction that they were no longer foreigners and outsiders, but Americans. The new consciousness and new possibilities caused the community to demand complete civil rights and full equality of opportunity. The American G.I. Forum, created to advocate this new goal, joined with LULAC to seek integration with all Americans, as Americans. Although Tejanos couched their rhetoric in patriotic terms, their tone was more insistent and more impatient. No longer would they tolerate the *de facto* Jim Crow system imposed upon them in the Lone Star State. *Are We Good Neighbors?* edited by Perales, voiced the new Tejano mentality.

However, the obstacles facing the intellectuals were formidable. The majority of Mexican Americans in San Antonio and throughout the Southwest were still mired in poverty and illiteracy. Segregation in housing, education, and the workplace continued to plague the community. Those who managed to overcome these obstacles, like Gus Garcia and Henry B. Gonzalez, often found themselves dogged by inner doubts that were the scars of years of discrimination.

In spite of these difficulties, Gonzalez became San Antonio's first Mexican-American congressman during a career dedicated to integrating Tejanos with the rest of the nation. Believing himself to be "an American of Mexican descent,"[102] he promoted a vision of a racially pluralistic America in all of his writings and speeches.

For this and other positions, Gonzalez came under criticism, not by Anglo segregationists but by young Tejanos who were part of the new Chicano movement. Chicanos like Jose Angel Gutierrez, Corky Gonzales, and Octavio Romano desired to establish a culturally and politically separate space for Mexican Americans in the Southwest, which they called Aztlán. The activists believed that modern post-industrial America was inherently oppressive and racist, and that separation was the only viable path to and personal and collective fulfillment. Chicanismo was most influential in the area of arts and culture, as Tejano artists interpreted their present and past through the lens of Chicano ideology. Their work attracted wide following, first among the Chicano community, then later among the general population.

The agenda of Chicanos, articulated through MAYO and La Raza Unida Party, did not have a lasting political hold on Tejanos in San Antonio. The Chicano Studies Movement was almost entirely a California phenomenon. Urban San Antonians did not identify with the ahistorical legend of Aztlán or with the agrarian emphasis of El Plan de Aztlán. Finally, Henry B. Gonzalez's opposition to the nationalist vision further impeded its influence. Yet, while voicing his disapproval of the Chicano understanding of community, he also spoke of the painful choices faced by individual Tejanos and Tejanas as they attempted to succeed in American society.

By the middle of the seventies, Mexican Americans in San Antonio were confronted with two competing visions of community and identity. One was the middle-class, integrationist paradigm of the Mexican-American generation. That vision emphasized individual mobility and participation in the American system; its values were taken primarily from American thought. Consciously or unconsciously, it was generally espoused by the growing middle-class, who benefited from jobs in the growing military economy, professions, and service industries.

Chicano activists constructed the other vision. They desired a linguistic, cultural, and even political separation from the U.S. whose values they questioned or rejected. Activists among the city's poor, its college campuses, and in the Winter Garden to the south were the main adherents of Chicanismo.

With the passing of time, the integrationist and Chicano identities would often compete, but would also sometimes complement one another. For example, as the baby boom generation and its children matured, they would often hold values about their culture and language consistent with

Chicanismo, while the same time having lifestyles that emphasized the individual and professional mobility that were championed by Mexican Americans. Just as the objectives and ideals of progressivism had differing affects on Mexican Americans in San Antonio and Los Angeles, Chicano ideology was also received in a dissimilar fashion.

Political perceptions also reflected this paradox. A new pride in Mexican heritage and culture now existed. Simultaneously, many Mexican Americans had an ambivalent attitude toward United States, made more ambivalent by the Vietnam War and the scandal of Watergate. While the memory of past and existing injustices lingered, Tejanos still believed in the American dream of possibilities for opportunity and justice. The return of many La Raza Unida activists to the Democratic Party in 1976 was partial proof of this new outlook.[103]

Ironically, as Mexican Americans and other minorities began making tangible gains toward approving their status as Americans, the very definition of American culture and what it meant to be an American became a matter of controversy and confusion within the society at large. A rethinking of American identity in the entire nation would present both opportunities and difficulties for the community. *Las mujeres*, Mexican-American women, would be most deeply affected by this controversy, and one of its most important participants.

Sandra Cisneros, Henry Cisneros, and the Postmodern Hispanic

On an afternoon in the historic King William District in downtown San Antonio, built by German immigrants in the nineteenth century, Sandra Cisneros, a writer of novels and short stories had lunch with a visitor, and identity was the topic of their discussion. Born in 1954, Cisneros has resided in San Antonio for the past 15 years.[1] By the time she moved to Texas, Cisneros had authored the bestselling novel *The House on Mango Street* and a number of other works having to do with the lives of Chicanos and Chicanas. Her life and work personified the subtle struggles of Mexican Americans, women and Americans in general. When she was asked how her life as a Mexican-American woman affected her work, she replied, "I feel like I've traveled and crossed many, many borders and cross them all the time, in a day."[2]

THE CHICANA FEMINIST DILEMMA

Cisneros stands on the shoulders of Mexican-American women who have played important parts in all facets of their history. As has been shown earlier, Juana Inés de la Cruz, Josefina Bright, Maria Latigo Hernandez, and Emma Tenayuca made critical contributions as the activists and intellectuals, seeking justice and equal opportunity. Mexican-American women in the Southwest figured prominently in labor strife in that area.[3] While the majority of leaders during the Mexican-American and early Chicano periods were male, women were indispensable at the grass roots. The Chicano movement saw an increase of female activism, both on the "street" level and on the intellectual front, as Chicanas were increasingly active as contributors to student newspapers.

As Chicanas began to enter colleges and universities with their brothers (albeit in very small numbers), they encountered a feminist movement that was gaining a larger voice during the sixties and early seventies. Energized by the civil rights effort and anti-Vietnam War protests, college educated

Anglo women attempted to expose and remove the barriers to social equality. Intellectuals such as Betty Friedan and Gloria Steinem argued that unequal relations between the sexes in the home and workplace were as great an injustice to women as slavery and segregation had been for blacks. As Chicanos argued for cultural independence from Anglos, feminists demanded economic and intellectual independence from men. This demand for independence challenged American assumptions about one of its most basic institutions, the family. Finally, the desire of feminists to be free of cultural taboos against women in the workforce created an emphasis on individualism within their movement, rather than a reliance on family or community. In fact, individualism was inherent in feminism from its earliest beginnings in the Transcendental movement and the 1848 Declaration of Sentiments. American feminists sought the power to determine their identity individually, not to have it placed on them by outside institutions. Today, many observers of feminism believe that this quest for self-actualization has become all-consuming. In 1998, Ginia Bellafonte asked the following question about the movement: "Want to know what today's chic young feminist thinkers care about? Their bodies! Themselves!"[4]

Mexican-American women believed themselves to be in a subservient position in the Chicano movement because of their exclusion from leadership and the movement's promotion of Indo-Mexican culture. Simultaneously, Chicanas distrusted the upper and middle class Anglo makeup of feminist organizations such as the National Organization for Women (NOW) due to Chicano nationalism. The content of their writing and action revealed a dual sense of alienation. According to Pesquera and Segura, "Chicana writings and organizational activities of this period resounded with frustration over patriarchy and Chicano Movement and a 'maternal chauvinism' in the women's movement. They sought various ways to reconcile the tension between cultural nationalism and feminism."[5] Rachel Madrigal summarized the situation of Chicana activists during the movement period: "First, she lives in a male-dominated American society; secondly, she is a Chicana living in an Anglo-dominated society; and thirdly, she is a young person living in a society controlled by middle-aged decisionmakers."[6]

While holding Anglo feminists at arm's length, Chicanas were in disagreement over the place of the traditional family and its effect on their freedom. Pesquera and Segura noted this dilemma when they said: "The Chicano movement exalted marriage and reproduction as integral to the politics of cultural reaffirmation. A fundamental feminist position, on the other hand, indicted marriage and reproduction within the traditional patriarchal family as a primary source of all women's subordination."[7] Some Chicanas believed that gender issues in the Mexican-American community were traceable to the discrimination against the entire community, and the condition of women would improve as the community was empowered. Enriqueta Longeaux y Vasquez of New Mexico advocated this belief when she wrote, "When the family is involved in a human rights movement, as is the Mexican-American family, there is little room for a women's liberation movement alone. The Mexican-American movement demands that, with the liberation of La Raza, we must have a total liberation. The woman must help liberate the man, and the man must look upon his liberation with the woman at his side, not behind him, following, but alongside of him, leading. The family must come up together."[8]

Other Chicanas felt that their personal freedom would never be achieved until they had economic and sexual independence from men, a belief that was more in tune with the Anglo feminism and that disagreed with the holistic vision put forth by Longeaux. Anna Nieto Gomez believed that in the economic sphere, "the woman should have . . . an equal position which is not dependent on fathers, husbands and sons. As long as she is economically dependent she will have to allow male privilege, to compromise herself."[9] The concept that "the personal is political,"[10] inherent in modern feminism, conflicted with the concept of collective memory that is a part of Chicano ideology and identity. Identity became a divisive issue for women, as it had for men during the 1927 meeting in Harlingen, Texas.

These disagreements came to the forefront on May 28–30, 1971 at the National Chicana Conference in Houston, Texas. The meeting was composed of 500 Chicanas, most of whom were young and college educated.[11] Activists who felt that the empowerment of the community was a more pressing issue than the liberation of women eventually left the conference. Those who remained issued the following statement: "With the involvement in the movement, marriage must change. Traditional roles are for Chicanas, no longer acceptable or applicable."[12]

Consequently, many Mexican-American women took up the feminist ethics of individualism and independence. Within some, the separatism of ethnicity was now coupled with a separatism of gender. The emerging Chicana Studies movement reflected this trend intellectually, as female scholars sought their own space apart from Mexican-American men and from Anglo society.[13] At the same time they were conscious of the triple identities that existed within them, that they were women existing in a cultural environment that was American and Mexican, and that they were heirs of a civilization that was European and Indian.

By the late 1980s, some Mexican thinkers began looking for a paradigm of identity based on the contradictions and paradoxes of their reality. The historian George J. Sanchez said that, "Any notion that individuals have occupied one undifferentiated cultural position–such as 'Mexican,' 'American' or 'Chicano'–has been abandoned in favor of the possibility of multiple identities and contradictory positions."[14] Echoing this sentiment was Austin feminist Martha Cotera, a former member of the La Raza Unida Party: "I hate this obsession which we have had since the start of our movement in the Sixties [sic] of 'The Chicano Search for Identity.' I don't think you have to search for your identity. You identify with one kind of feeling at one point, and then another and another, in a process of refinement."[15] As early as 1977 Rachel Madrigal embraced this new individualized, eclectic identity when she said "The individual [Chicana] may identify herself with aspects of the Chicano culture and heritage as seem valuable to her, and is able to identify positively with these values."[16] On the other hand, the Chicana could also reject those aspects of Mexican culture which have a negative impact on her as a member of postmodern America.

Chicanas had now become part of the American mindset that permitted its members to invent and reinvent themselves at their choosing. Sandra Cisneros' character Esperanza in *House on Mango Street* was a type of this kind of reinvention. The publisher wrote, "Esperanza doesn't want to belong—not to her rundown neighborhood, and not to the low expectations the world has for her. Esperanza's story is that of a young girl coming into her power, and inventing for herself what she will become."[17] The existential exercise of inventing oneself from oneself could be likened to building a bridge from a cliff, not seeing the other side. Yet that would be the project of Cisneros and other Chicana feminists.

As a Latina artist and writer, Sandra Cisneros is in search of a home. Comparing herself to her Tejano neighbors, she said that, "I've moved not only geographically but with education, the feminist movement, and up and down between classes, because I'm an artist and I'd been invited into salons and homes and other places that most people wouldn't be invited. It's a completely different sense of identity than my neighbors. But the awards, my education, especially my art and my success have allowed me to be more mobile, but not necessarily at home! Welcomed, but not at home." When asked where she felt at home, Cisneros replied: "I don't feel at home anywhere, I'm kind of homeless, in a sense."[18]

The west central community in Chicago where Sandra grew up[19] was very different from the Southwest, most particularly in the ways that Mexicans related to other races. Manuel Gonzales observed that "Mexicans residing in the Midwest had experience which differed significantly from their compatriots living in the border area. Midwestern Mexicans were less isolated from outsiders, often living and working with European populations."[20] Drawn to these regions by the lure of industrial jobs, Mexican immigrants in cities like Chicago formed their own ethnic enclave, as did the Irish, Italians and many others. At the same time, there was space in the city in which all groups intermingled on a regular basis. Sandra observed about this, "You could hear Ukrainian, Polish, Puerto Rican Spanish, Mexican Spanish, and hillbilly English on the same bus. But that kind of community allowed me to have my dual identity of being Mexican and American simultaneously, so when I said [I was] Mexican in English I didn't have to add the American part. It was understood, because I said it in English."[21] In cities like Chicago, Mexican immigrants were part of the same ethnically pluralistic "melting pot," their social status was nearly equal with Europeans. Cisneros noted about her childhood that, "in Chicago, everybody was something." However, in Texas, where Tejanos were marginalized because of their skin color, and in California, where Chicanos were marginalized because of their language, their existential and intellectual experience was more like that of blacks.

As a result of relative ethnic equality, issues of class in Chicago were least as great as those created by race. Cisneros remarked that, "there was a moment for me where those 'glimmers' I had felt in Chicago, when you walk down Michigan Avenue and wondered why you didn't dress right, you got those 'glimmers' of [being] less than, or again in the Field Museum, standing next to some woman picking up her fur coat at the coat check, you got those glimmers of shame and you think 'why didn't I dress up more' but it wasn't about clothes, it was about money."[22]

Cisneros' sense of alienation came most vividly into view when she became a graduate student at the University of Iowa, during a literary seminar when students were required to write about their childhood homes. Sandra noticed immediately that the stories of the other students, who were mostly Anglo middle and upper-class, were very different from the working class environment she had grown up in. This sense of difference resulted in shame that turned into rage, rage that would later produce Cisneros' first literary achievement, *The House on Mango Street*. The book emerged from an epiphany that occurred as she worked through her feelings. In the introduction, she wrote that "When I recognized the places where I departed from my neighbors, my classmates, my family, my town, my brothers, when I discovered that I knew what no one else in the room [sic] and then speak it in a voice that was my voice . . . Then I could speak, shout, laugh from a place that was uniquely mine, that was no one else's in the history of the universe, that would never be anyone else's, ever."[23] Later, she would say of that time, "I started writing about my neighborhood to distance myself from my classmates. It was a self-ghettoization, but it was a ghettoization of choice, because I wanted to write about something they could not."[24] Where Juana Inés de la Cruz wrote from an outsider position assigned her by Mexican society, Cisneros wrote from an outsider status she created for herself.

Throughout her career, Sandra Cisneros has written from a place of alienation, solitude, and difference, a position reminiscent of Henry Thoreau, Emily Dickinson, and Henry Adams. The protagonists in her writings make up a list of the dispossessed in society—namely women from dysfunctional or disempowered situations, homosexuals, and others at the lower and of the social scale, all of them from Mexican-American society. Another theme of her writing is that people will lie and tell fictitious stories about themselves to be accepted or to deal with the gray dreariness of their lives. Life is often depicted in its most private detail, resulting in a recurrence of the hidden and obscene corners of existence. An example is *Woman Hollering Creek*, her collection of short stories, many of which consist of ribald banter and gossip between Chicanas. One such selection was entitled *La Fabulosa: A Texas Operetta.* There, the narrator related: "She kept this corporal at Fort Sam Houston. Young. A looker. José Arrambide. He had a high school honey back home who sold nachos at the mall, still waiting for him to come back to Harlingen, marry her, and buy that three-piece bedroom set on layaway. Dream on, right?"[25]

Cisneros' use of storytelling is a typically Mexican device, but the individualistic and postmodern content of her stories is typically American. In her life and writing she attempts to solve the problem of ethnic identity in the same way that Roger Williams worked out his religious identity in the seventeenth century; by individualizing it.

When Sandra Cisneros moved to San Antonio, she immediately encountered criticism because of cultural misunderstandings, both with the larger community of San Antonio and its Tejano population. The most publicized dispute occurred over how Sandra and Tejanos related to Mexico and their common Mexican past. "I never understood 'Mexican' as a pejorative term until I moved here," Cisneros told the author. "Mexican was good. That allowed me to do audacious acts, what others considered audacious but I just considered my right because I was born with that sense of entitlement of being Mexican."[26]

So there was cultural conflict, even though Cisneros and the Tejano community had common origins in Mexico. Those origins, however, were filtered through divergent experiences in the U.S., one living in an ethnically egalitarian environment in a northern city, the other having a heritage in the southern racial caste system. Each experience produced a different mentality about the Mexican and American experiences.

Another example of cultural difficulties encountered by Cisneros took place after she painted her home a bright purple. Although that color is popular for homes in Mexico, it was not architecturally consistent with the neighborhood's history, which was Victorian German. Members of the King William Association protested to San Antonio city staff that Cisneros' individualism was detrimental to the historical ambiance of the community. She replied, "According to my history, purple is a historical color . . . this was Mexico, and the Mexican color palette isn't being allowed."[27] Although compromise was reached, Cisneros pointed out that the incident was one of many that branded her, a Mexican-American feminist, as an outsider. She told me, "I think, how many years later, I'm still an anomaly. I still am, you know. I still make those blunders that come out of . . . my forgetting that Mexican is supposed to be bad."[28]

Sandra Cisneros, a self-described "Buddha-lupana" (a Buddhist tied to the symbols of her Mexican history)[29] is typical of the postmodern intellectual who has crossed borders of class, race, and gender without completely committing to any one place. She is also representative of the Latina feminist who chooses to identify herself with the most edifying experiences of her life and the world around her. She concluded lunch with her visitor by observing, "So you see I've crossed a lot of borders to come to the place where I feel at home."[30] Seventeen years later, she is still Esperanza, living on Mango Street.

HENRY CISNEROS AND COPS

Unlike Sandra Cisneros, Henry Cisneros (1947–, no relation) San Antonio's first Mexican-American mayor of the twentieth century, had roots deep in the city's history. His maternal grandfather, Romulo Mungia, came to San Antonio, started a printing business, and joined the group of Mexican exiles centered around *La Prensa*. Henry was a scholastic overachiever, graduating with a Master of Urban Planning degree in 1970 from Texas A&M University, and receiving his doctorate from George Washington University in 1975.[31]

Henry was elected to the San Antonio City Council in that same year, the youngest person ever elected to that body. Six years later, he was elected mayor. Very quickly he assumed a position of national visibility, a symbol of the new Mexican American, who no longer thought of himself as an outsider. According to Richard Garcia, "Cisneros, above all, exemplified the rise of the Mexican American generation and the search for . . . its identity."[32]

A number of changes in San Antonio politics made the success of Henry Cisneros possible. One of the most important of these was the creation of a new kind of political activism. Calling the city leadership's attention to long-neglected needs was the purpose for founding Communities Organized for Public Service [COPS] in 1974. Most of those needs were focused on the indigent sections of San Antonio and among the Mexican-American community.

COPS was distinctive from earlier activism in a number of important respects. First, its goals were practical reform of immediate issues, such as drainage, utility rates, and the allocation of city services. In addition, the basis of the group was institutional, rather than personal, as was the case with La Raza Unida.[33] The institutional focus was the result of the organizing principles of Saul Alinsky, who specialized in raising the consciousness of local communities to inequities in their area, than in educating them on how to remedy those inequities.

Another important feature of COPS was its connection to the Catholic Church. One of the group's founders was Father Albert Benavides, a local priest. He and other clergy held important positions of leadership within COPS, and nearly all chapters held their meetings on the grounds of Catholic parishes. According to Beatrice Gomez, "We have a strong sense of family and of neighborhood, and we wanted to improve the conditions where we live. The Church gave us the strength we needed to try."[34] As the members of the G.I. Forum had political credibility because of their veteran status, COPS had credibility in the Mexican-American community because of its religious affiliation. Also, the organization was committed to making improvements and reforms by working through the system, as had LULAC and the Forum.

Peter Skerry also noted how COPS was a bilingual organization. He said, "Language use reveals how [COPS] deals with identity. Spanish can be an important part of day-to-day life in the stable Mexican-American [sic] neighborhoods targeted by Alinsky organizers. Yet organizers [also] teach that 'English is the language of power.'"[35] Because of the use of the English language, its institutional focus, and willingness to work within the American governmental system, COPS gave the Mexican-American community an education in American citizenship, even as they were loudly and vigorously protesting against their exclusion from that system. What is intriguing about COPS was that it took the approach that if the community was improved, all of its members benefited. As a result of its activism, it empowered Tejanos and Tejanas without the singular focus of identity organization.

In an interview near the end of her life, Emma Tenayuca noted about COPS, "[I]t's the women who have led. And I just have a feeling, a very strong feeling, that if ever this world is civilized, it will be more the work of women."[36] From the founding of COPS women were part of its leadership and organization. Beatriz Gallego decided to become involved when her South San Antonio street became a river during the flood of 1973.[37] Looking back on six years as a member of COPS, Gallego said, "The most important change (wrought by the group) is in people. Everybody feels much better about themselves."[38] Successes in changing the community, therefore, also gave it self-confidence.

Political organization, education, and a newly instilled sense of confidence were the key factors in electing Henry Cisneros mayor in April 1981. As a city councilman, Cisneros appeared to be the embodiment of the aspirations held by the Mexican-American community. Imbued with the values of both of the Mexican Catholic identity and the American work ethic, he seemed the prototype of the modern Mexican American, able to stand on an equal basis with anyone in the nation. In 1976, he professed a commitment both to the community and to the need for individual opportunity by saying that "Over the last decade generations of Mejicanos [sic] have worked their fingers and shoulders raw and driven themselves to premature old age in order that their sons and daughters could take their rightful places in society. That legacy of sweat and tears provides a moral imperative that this generation assert itself to fulfill its most sacred dreams." Continuing, he said that, "We have before us a generation of men and women who are hungry for what they can achieve as only those who have been barred from the table can be hungry."[39] While Cisneros acknowledged his debt to the collective consciousness of Mexican identity, his rhetoric contained echoes of Franklin D. Roosevelt and John F. Kennedy–of a torch being passed to a new generation. It was an American vision, drawn from Mexican memories.

The eight-year mayoralty of Cisneros was dominated, in his own words, by the twin priorities of "Ethnically and racially inclusive decision-making, matched to continuing economic growth and progress."[40] In doing so, however, he had to navigate through both city politics, where COPS and similar groups had grown increasingly powerful, and through the demands of a national political and economic structure. In short, Cisneros became an American politician. Although the rhetoric of his earlier career appealed to the Mexican-American sense of community, his policies became geared toward Ronald Reagan's America of economic and cultural individualism. Cisneros brought San Antonio into the world that was feared by Henry B. Gonzalez, condemned by Jose Angel Gutierrez, but (culturally, at least) welcomed by Sandra Cisneros and Latina feminists. According to Richard Garcia, "Cisneros could now answer the question asked by Juan Solis in the 1920s after returning home from World War I: What are we, Mexicans or Americans? Cisneros could now respond, 'We are Americans, but distinct individuals as well who can *choose* [emphasis mine] to maintain a memory of Mexican collectivity, or simply, as in San Antonio, to exist in the reality of *lo mexicano*.'"[41]

In different ways, author Sandra Cisneros and politician Henry Cisneros illustrate the important shift in conceiving of Mexican-American identity, and the nature of American identity itself. Whereas in the past, individual identity was prescribed either by family, community, or the larger society and its institutions, identity for postmodern Americans corresponds to David Riesman's autonomous personality in an other-directed environment, where the individual is free to define himself or herself according to their own tastes and desires.[42]

At the same time, Tejano identity was now being molded by exogenous forces—with other Mexican-American communities in the Southwest and Midwest, each with their own culture and historical experiences; with Cubans, Puerto Ricans, other Spanish-speaking ethnic groups; finally, San Antonio was becoming more and more interwoven with overall American culture. All these new contacts were the result of technological innovations of the past fifty years, especially the ubiquitous influence of television. In many ways, Mexican Americans throughout the nation are experiencing the ahistorical culture present in Los Angeles.

So, while many Mexican Americans felt greater freedom to form the borders of their individual identities, they saw their collective identity being threatened with homogenization within a Hispanic identity based on language, or feared being swept into the American melting pot. Also, a number of national trends make the preservation of community problematic. The breakup of the traditional family and trends of corporate organization that transfer employees hundreds and even thousands of miles from their birthplace are among these. This is especially troubling because of the central role that the extended family and physical place have had in the shaping of the Mexican consciousness. Mexican Americans are seeking to maintain their values in the midst of these new phenomena are reshaping the ideas of family, community, and nationality. If they are to be successful, according to COPS founder Ernesto Cortes, "they will have to have the security that comes with confidence in their own identity and history."[43]

A sense of historical tradition is critical to a living awareness of identity. Human beings can endure almost any circumstances, the worst forms of exclusion, discrimination, and even genocide as long as they are aware of their significance in this space-time continuum of history. Recent theories in literary criticism and historiography have called into question the reality of historical meaning. Far from empowering minorities, this is a form of cultural genocide, because it severs them from a collective consciousness. We are as linked to history as we are biologically connected to our ancestors though the DNA in our bodies. The mapping of the human genome has interesting implications for those trying to gain an understanding of the past, especially the past of minority groups and women.

Historical literacy gives minorities an assurance of their identity, and can protect them from the sort of manipulation that was attempted by Anglo progressives in California during the Progressive period. Mass society and the media would tend to reduce all groups to their lowest common cultural denominator. Paradoxically, history can educate not only for difference but also to the interdependence of all humans on one another, reducing ignorance, prejudice and distrust. In the history of Mexicans run the culture of the Roman, Christian, Moslem Moor, Native American, and African American. Mexican Americans are uniquely suited to bridge divides of culture, race and gender. They are living demonstrations of what Martin Luther King, Jr. asserted when he wrote "We are tied together in the simple garment of destiny, caught in the inescapable network of mutuality."[44]

Appendix

To develop within the members of our race the best, purest, and most perfect type of a true and loyal citizen of the United States of America.

To eradicate from our body politic all intents and tendencies to establish discriminations among our fellow citizens on account of race, religion our social position as being contrary to the true spirit of Democracy, our Constitution, and our Laws.

To use all legal means at our command to the end that all citizens in our country may enjoy equal rights, the equal protection of the laws of the land, and equal opportunities and privileges.

The acquisition of the English language, which is the official language of our country, being necessary for the enjoyment of our rights and privileges, we declare it to be the official language of this organization and we pledge ourselves to learn and speak the same to our children.

To define with absolute and unmistakable clearness our unquestionable loyalty to the principles, ideals, and citizenship of the United States of America.

To assume complete responsibility for the education of our children as to their rights and duties and the language and customs of this country; the latter, in so far as they may be good customs.

We solemnly declare once and for all to maintain a sincere and respectful reverence for our racial origin, of which we are proud.

Secretly and openly, by all lawful means at our command, we shall assist in the education and guidance of Latin-Americans [sic] and we shall protect and defend their lives and interests whenever necessary.

We shall destroy any attempt to create racial prejudices against our people, and any infamous stigma which may be cast upon them, and we shall demand for them the respect and prerogatives which the Constitution grants to us all.

Each of us considers himself with equal responsibilities in our organization, to which we voluntarily swear subordination and obedience.

We shall create a fund for our mutual protection, for the defense of those of us who may be unjustly prosecuted, and for the education and culture of our people.

This organization is not a political club, but as citizens we shall participate in all local, state, and national political contests. However, in doing so we shall ever bear in mind the general welfare of our people; and we disregard and abjure for all in any personal obligation that are not in harmony with these principles.

With our vote influence we shall endeavor to place in public office men who show by their conduct respect and consideration for our people.

We shall select as our leaders those among us who demonstrate, by their integrity and culture, that they are capable of guiding and directing us properly.

We shall maintain public means for the diffusion of these principles and the expansion and consolidation of this organization.

We shall pay our poll tax, and that of the members of our families, in order that we may enjoy our rights fully.

We shall diffuse our ideas by means of the press, lectures, and pamphlets.

Notes

NOTES TO CHAPTER ONE

1. Octavio Páz, *The Labyrinth of Solitude: Life and Thought in Mexico* trans. Lysander Kemp (New York: Grove Press, 1961), 20.
2. Samuel S. Buck, *Yanaguana's Successors*, (San Antonio: R.M. Benavides, 1980), 67.
3. Jesus de la Teja, *San Antonio: A City on New Spain's Far Northern Frontier* (Albuquerque: University of New Mexico Press, 1995), xi.
4. John Bierhorst, trans. *History and Mythology of the Aztecs: The Codex Chimalpopoca,* (Tucson: University of Arizona Press, 1992), 1.
5. Victor-Mendoza-Grado, comp. "Codex Mendoza" <http://www.ironhorse.com/~nagual/codex>.
6. As noted earlier, the practice of destroying earlier histories was not unique to the Europeans. Bierhorst, 1.
7. Numerous monographs and articles have been written on Indigenous thought and philosophy before the Conquest. See Miguel León-Portilla, *Aztec Thought and Culture: The Study of the Ancient Nahuatl Mind* trans. Jack Emory Davis (Norman: University of Oklahoma Press, 1969).
8. León-Portilla, *The Study of the Nahuatl Mind,* 9ff.
9. Bernardino de Sahagún, *A General History of the Things of New Spain; The Florentine Codex.* (Santa Fe, N.M.: School of American Research, 1975), Book 6, Chapter 10, 51 and Leon-Portilla, *Aztec Thought and Culture,* 121–124.
10. Páz, *Labyrinth of Solitude,* 20.
11. Páz, *The Labyrinth of Solitude,* 10–11.
12. See John Winthrop, "A Modell of Christian Charity" contained in *The Puritans: A Sourcebook of their Writings* ed. Perry Miller and Thomas H. Johnson (New York: Harper and Row, 1938), 195–99. Winthrop's view of the individual in seventeenth century Puritan New England society was similar to that held by Mexica and later Mexican culture.

13. Manuel Orozco y Berra, Introduction to Fernando de Alba Ixtlilxochitl, *Ally of Cortés: Account 13, Of the Coming of the Spaniards and the Beginning of the Evangelical Law* trans. Douglas K. Ballantine (El Paso: Texas Western Press, 1969), xxii.

14. Manuel G. Gonzales, *Mexicanos: a History of Mexicans in the United States* (Bloomington: Indiana University Press, 1999), 36.

15. To understand the intellectual and spiritual interaction of Aztec and Spanish thought in greater detail, see Robert Ricard, *The Spiritual Conquest of Mexico: An Essay on the Apostalate and Evangelizing Methods of the Mendicant orders in New Spain 1523–1572,* trans. Lesley Byrd Simpson (Berkeley: University of California, 1966), Benjamin Keen, *The Aztec Image in Western Thought* (New Brunswick: Rutgers University Press, 1990); Louise M. Burkhart, *The Slippery Earth: Nahua-Christian Moral Dialogue in Sixteenth-Century Mexico* (Tucson: University of Arizona Press, 1989).

16. Gomez-Quiñoñes, *Roots of Chicano Politics,* 17.

17. Gonzales, *Mexicanos,* 27.

18. Gomez-Quiñoñes, *Roots of Chicano Politics,* 13.

19. Fernando de Alba Ixtlilxochitl, *Ally of Cortés,* 84.

20. Alberto Ruy-Sánchez, "The Problem of Mexican Identity" in *Identities in North America: The Search for Community* ed. Robert L Earle and John D. Wirth (Stanford, Cal.: Stanford University Press, 1995), 40.

21. Páz, *The Labyrinth of Solitude,* 20.

22. Juana Inés de la Cruz, *A Woman of Genius: The Intellectual Autobiography of Sor Juana Inés de la Cruz* trans. Margaret Sayers Peden (Salisbury, Connecticut: Lime Rock Press, 1982), 66. "pues todas no fueron más que mujeres doctas, tenidas y celebradas y también veneradas de la antiguedad por tales."

23. George H. Tavard, *Juana Ines de la Cruz and the Theology of Beauty: The First Mexican Theology* (Notre Dame: University of Notre Dame Press, 1991), 188. See also Jonathan Edwards, *The Nature of True Virtue* (1765).

24. Henry Bierck, ed. Selected Writings of Bolivar, Vol. 1.

25. Religion and religious symbolism plays a critical part in the development of Mexican and Mexican American thought. See Callcott, *Church and State in Mexico.* This important trend will be discussed in greater detail later.

26. Bernard Bailyn, *The Ideological Origins of the American Revolution* (Cambridge, Mass.: Belknap Press, 1967), 34–54.

27. Gomez-Quiñoñes, *Roots of Chicano Politics,* 101.

28. Willfrid Hardy Callcott, *Church and State in Mexico, 1822–1857* (New York: Octagon Books, 1971), 53.

29. Ibid.

30. The identity and consciousness of persons of Mexican descent in Texas is distinct from that of other parts of the Southwest. The ethnic designation Tejano will be used, rather than Chicano, which is primarily a Southern California appellation, except in those instances where the Chicano movement is being particularly discussed.

31. Richard A. Garcia, *Rise of the Mexican American Middle Class,* 307.

32. Eugene Rodriguez, Jr. "Henry B. Gonzalez: A Political Profile" (Master's Thesis, St. Mary's University, 1965), 9–10.

33. Matovina, *Tejano Religion and Ethnicity*, 227.

34. de la Teja, *San Antonio De Bexar*, 24–25.

35. Buck, *Yanaguana's Successors*.

36. Matovina, *Tejano Religion and Ethnicity*, 25.

37. de la Teja, 152.

38. Matovina, *Tejano Religion and Ethnicity*, 99, n7.

39. Jose Maria Sanchez, "A Trip to Texas in 1828," trans. Carlos E. Castañeda, *Southwestern Historical Quarterly* 29 (April 1926): 270–281, quoted in David J. Weber, *Foreigners in their Native Land* (Albuquerque: University of New Mexico Press 1973), 83. It is worthy of reiteration that this slight, which could not have been accidental, took place while Texas was a part of Mexico, and that Sanchez was a member of the Mexican government.

40. Ibid, 81. For another opinion of the quality of Anglo immigrants to Texas, see the observations of Abbé Emmanuel Domenech in Montejano, *Anglos and Mexicans*, 31–32.

41. Arnoldo De Leon, "White Racial Attitudes toward Mexicanos in Texas, 1821–1900" (Doctoral Dissertation, Texas Christian University 1947), 29.

42. See Montejano, *Anglos and Mexicans*, 312–313, for an interpretation of both haciendas and plantations as instruments of capitalism that retained the trappings of aristocracy.

43. Everett Dick, *The Dixie Frontier: A Social History of the Southern Frontier from the First Transmontane Beginnings to The Civil War* (New York: Knopf, 1948), 85.

44. Ibid.

45. By 1836 Anglos outnumbered Tejanos four to one. Samuel H. Lowrie, *Culture Conflict in Texas, 1821–1835* (New York: AMS Press, 1967), 31.

46. For information regarding relations between Anglo-Americans and Tejanos see Arnoldo De Leon, "White Racial Attitudes;" *They Called Them Greasers: Anglo Attitudes toward Mexicans in Texas, 1821–1900* (Austin: University of Texas Press, 1983) Acuna, *Occupied America*, Montejano, *Anglos and Mexicans in the Making of Texas*.

47. Montejano, *Anglos and Mexicans*, 223–24.

48. De Leon, "White Racial Attitudes," 135–36.

49. Glen E. Lich, *The German Texans* (San Antonio: University of Texas Institute of Texan Cultures, 1981), 91, 94, 97.

50. Ibid, 35. However much whites may have expressed a revulsion of racial mixture, such mixture was common and easily documented, with Native Americans, blacks and Mexicans.

51. Montejano, *Anglos and Mexicans*, 194.

52. Congress, House, Congressman James Hammond, 35th Congress, 1st sess. *Congressional Globe* (March 9, 1858), Appendix, 71.

53. Robert Blauner, *Racial Oppression in America* (New York: Harper and Row, 1972), 27.

54. Ibid, 142.

55. Ibid, 145.

56. Acuña, *Occupied America*, 28.

57. De Leon, "White Racial Attitudes," 145.

58. Matovina, *Tejano Ethnicity*, 79.

59. Lich, *The German Texans*, 43.

60. Chester W. and Ethel Geue, *A New Land Beckoned: German Immigration to Texas, 1844–47* (Waco: Texian Press, 1972), 2.

61. Lich, *The German Texans*, 124.

62. Frederick Law Olmsted, *Journey through Texas, or A Saddle-Trip on the Southwestern Frontier* (New York: Dix, Edwards & Co., 1857), 164–65.

63. Matovina, 25.

64. David C. Weber, ed. *Foreigners in Their Native Land: Historical Roots of the Mexican Americans* (Albuquerque: University of New Mexico Press, 1973), 177.

65. Juan N. Seguín, *Personal Memoirs of Juan N. Seguín, from the Year 1834 to the Retreat of General Woll from San Antonio, 1842* (San Antonio, 1858) in Weber, *Foreigners*, 178.

66. It would be intriguing to research why the writings of Seguín, which were in English, and the translated works of other Mexican Americans such as Juan Cortina did not receive as wide circulation in the Anglo community as did Douglass and other black slaves.

67. Weber, 177.

68. Montejano, *Anglos and Mexicans*, 29.

69. Matovina, 46.

70. "Esparza Remembers" in Driggs and King, eds. *Rise of the Lone Star*, 214–215, in Matovina, 45–46.

71. Guadalupe San Miguel, *Let All of Them Take Heed: Mexican Americans and the Campaign for Racial Equality in Texas, 1910–1981* (Austin: University of Texas Press, 1987), 13.

72. Acuña, *Occupied America*, 239.

73. Walter Prescott Webb, *The Texas Rangers* (Cambridge: Harvard University Press, 1935), 175–76, in Americo Paredes, *With a Pistol in His Hand: A Border Ballad and its Hero* (Austin: University of Texas Press, 1958), 31.

74. Psalm Chapter 137, verse 1.

75. Paredes, *With a Pistol in His Hand*, 169.

76. Ibid, 113.

77. Ibid, 242.

NOTES TO CHAPTER TWO

1. Thomas Bender, *Intellect and the Public Life: Essays On The Social History of Academic Intellectuals In The United States*, (Baltimore: Johns Hopkins University Press, 1993), 5.

2. David A. Hollinger, *In the American Province: Studying the History and the Historiography of Ideas*, (Bloomington: Indiana University Press, 1985), 134.

3. Mario T. Garcia, *Mexican Americans: Leadership, Ideology and Identity, 1930–1960*, (New Haven: Yale University Press, 1989), 15.

4. Mario T. Garcia, *Mexican Americans*, 15–16.

5. Adela Sloss-Vento, *Alonso S. Pereles: His Struggle for the Rights of Mexican Americans*, Introduction by Arnold C. Vento, (San Antonio, Texas: Artes Graphicas, 1977). Richard A. Garcia, *Rise of the Mexican American Middle Class*, San Antonio 1929–1941 Forward by Henry C. Schmidt, (College Station: Texas A&M University Press, 1991), 354.

6. Richard A. Garcia, *Rise of the Mexican American Middle Class*, 268.

7. Marta Cotera, *The Profile of the Mexican American Woman*, (Austin: Information Systems Development, 1976), 68.

8. William Beezley, "San Antonio: Capital of Insurgent Mexico" in *SALAM and the Area Studies Community: Papers of the Thirty-Seventh Annual Meeting of the Seminar on the Acquisition of Latin American Library Materials, Nettie Lee Benson Latin American Collection, University of Texas at Austin, Austin Texas, May 30-June 4, 1992*, ed. David Block (Albuquerque: SALAM Secretariat, General Library, University Of New Mexico, 1994), 45.

9. Manuel G. Gonzales, *Mexicanos*, 113.

10. Manuel Ruiz Ibañez, "Spanish-Language Press Had a Vital Role in San Antonio History," *San Antonio Express*, (June 18, 1972).

11. Ruben Munguia, *La Prensa*, (San Antonio: Universidad Nacional de Mexico, 1987), 2.

12. "A la Prensa, a nuestros amigos y al publico," *La Prensa*, (February 13, 1913), 1.

13. Mungia, 2.

14. Frank Pinedo, "A Life That's Worth Living," *LULAC News* 21(February 1954): 43.

15. Jose Amaro Hernandez, *Mutual Aid for Survival: the Case of the Mexican American*. (Malabar, FL, Robert E. Krieger Publishing Co., 1983), 62, 64, n16.

16. Stuart J. Barnes, "Bitterness On The Border," in *Are We Good Neighbors?* Ed. Alonso Pereles (San Antonio, TX: Artes Graphicas, 1948), 81.

17. Montejano, *Anglos and Mexicans*, 117–120.

18. Ibid, 181.

19. Richard A. Garcia, "The Making of the Mexican American Mind, San Antonio, Texas 1929–1940" (Ph.D. Dissertation, University of California at Irvine, 1980), 105.

20. Ibid.

21. Cynthia E. Orozco, "The Origins of the League of United Latin American Citizens (LULAC) and the Mexican American Civil Rights Movement in Texas, with an Analysis of Women's Political Participation in a Gendered Context," (Ph.D. Dissertation, University of California at Los Angeles, 1992), 123.

22. Hernandez, *Mutual Aid*, 75.

23. Ibid, 66.

24. Orozco, "Beyond Machismo, La Familia, and Ladies' Auxiliaries: a Historiography of Mexican-Origin Women's Participation in Voluntary Associations

and Politics in the United States, 1870–1990," *Perspectives in Mexican American Studies* 5(1995): 13.

25. George J. Sanchez and Julie Lenninger Pycior have both commented on why the institutional Catholic Church was not a socialization agent for Mexican American men. See *Becoming Mexican American*, 152, 165 and LBJ and *Mexican Americans: The Paradox of Power*, (Austin: University of Texas Press, 1997), 202.

26. Hernandez, *Mutual Aid*, 64 n16.

27. Orozco, "Origins of LULAC."

28. Richard Garcia, *Rise of the Middle Class*, 255.

29. J. Luz Saenz, "Racial Discrimination: the Number One Problem in Texas Schools," in *Are We Good Neighbors?*, 33.

30. Orozco, "Origins of LULAC" 177–78.

31. Richard Garcia, *Rise of the Middle Class*, 269; Orozco, "Origins of LULAC;" interview with Ruben Mungia, May 8, 1999.

32. Sanchez, *Becoming Mexican American*, 3–4.

33. Matovina, 84–88.

34. Orozco, "Origins of LULAC," 242–243, 245.

35. George J. Garza, "Founding and History of LULAC, League of United Latin American Citizens," *LULAC News* 21(February 1954):21.

36. Adolf A. Garza, "Citizenship," *LULAC News* 1 (August 1931):5.

37. Ibid.

38. "Aims and Purposes of LULAC" *LULAC News* 1 (August 1931):3–4.

39. Richard Garcia, *Rise of the Mexican American Middle Class*, 260.

40. Ibid.

41. Ibid, 269.

42. Paula S. Foss, Outside *in: Minorities and the Transformation of American Education* (New York: Oxford University Press,) 40, in Orozco, "Origins of LULAC," 112.

43. Montejano, *Anglos and Mexicans*, 234.

44. Acuña, *Occupied America*, 239.

45. Malcolm Ross, "Our Personal Placements with Mexican Americans," in Perales, *Are We Good Neighbors?* 73. Richard Garcia also pointed out that "LULAC, like the ricos, carried with its cultural and intellectual ideas the emotions of an elite, but the sensitivity of noblesse oblige. LULAC felt comfortable, therefore, with the patrician and aristocratic tone and temper exhibited by Franklin D. Roosevelt and his use of Hamiltonian means to achieve Jeffersonian ends." Richard Garcia, *Rise of the Middle Class*, 281.

46. Robert C. Hammerback, Richard J. Jensen and Jose Angel Gutierrez, *War of Words: Chicano Context and the 1960s and 1970s* (Westport, Connecticut: Greenwood Press, 1985), 140–41.

47. San Miguel, *Let All of Them Take Heed*, 70.

48. Richard Garcia, *Rise of the Middle Class*, 258.

49. Bender, *Intellect and the Public Life*, 80.

50. Richard Garcia, *Rise of the Middle Class*, 296.

51. Ibid, 294.

52. Alonso S. Perales, "La Evolucíon de la Raza Mexicana en Texas," *La Prensa*, September 13, 1927, 1.

53. Orozco, "Origins of LULAC," 288–90.

54. Perales, "La Evolucíon de la Raza," 1.

55. This author believes that the polarity between the Mexican exiles and the Tejano middle class created by Richard Garcia was overstated. They collaborated in a number of arenas. Garcia himself admitted that in spite of the divergent national to focus of each group, "[in] watching them in their socio-cultural environment, one could not tell the difference [between them]." "Mexican American Middle Class," 216.

56. Alonso Perales, *En Defensa de Mi Raza*, vol. 1, (San Antonio: Artes Graficas, 1937), 28–29.

57. Perales, *En Defensa de Mi Raza*, vol. 2, 33.

58. *The Handbook of Texas Online*, (http://www.tsha.utexas.edu/handbook/online/search.html) June 14, 2000, "Gonzales, Manuel C." by Cynthia E. Orozco.

59. Orozco, "Origins of LULAC," 200–201.

60. *The Handbook of Texas Online*, s.v. "Mexican Protective League."

61. It should be reiterated that the concept of identity within Mexico was changing at the very time Mexican Americans were struggling with the issue in the U.S.

62. Orozco, "Origins of LULAC," 201.

63. Ibid, 238–239, 242; in fact, Gonzales served as the Consul General's representative at the convention.

64. Orozco, "Origins of LULAC,"258, n.80.

65. Richard Garcia, *Rise of the Middle Class*, 293.

66. Pycior, *LBJ and Mexican Americans*, 146.

67. "LULAC Through the Years: History of Former LULAC Presidents," *LULAC News* 21 (February 1954):65.

68. *Independent School District v. Salvatierra*, 33 S.W. 2nd 790 (1930).

69. Antonio Castaño, "Flowers to the Living," *LULAC News*, 1 (November 1931):13–14.

70. M.C. Gonzales, "Echoes of the Kingsville Convention," *LULAC News* 1 (September 1931):8.

71. Ibid.

72. "Aims and Purposes of LULAC," *LULAC News* 1(August 1931): 1.

73. Ibid, 317.

74. Ibid, 300, 321.

NOTES TO CHAPTER THREE

1. Julia Kirk Blackwelder, *Women in the Depression: Cast and Culture in San Antonio, 1929–39*, (College Station, Texas: Texas A&M University Press, 1984), 168.

2. Blackwelder,18.

3. Geoffrey Rips, "Emma Tenayuca: Alive and Well in San Antonio," *San Antonio Women's Magazine* 2 (April 1985), 8.

4. Ibid.

5. Richard Garcia, *Mexican American Middle Class*, 26–29.

6. Seldon C. Manefee and Orin C. Cassmore, *Pecan Shellers: The Problems of Underpaid and Unemployed Mexican Labor*, (Washington, D.C. GPO, 1940), 43.

7. Blackwelder,150.

8. Ibid, 177–78,184.

9. Emma Tenayuca and Homer Brooks, "The Mexican Question in the Southwest" *The Communist* 1 (March 1939): 258.

10. Ibid, 258–59.

11. Tenayuca and Brooks, 262.

12. Ibid, 266.

13. Arthur Koestler, *The God That Failed*, ed. Richard Crossman (New York: Harper and Brothers, 1949), 62.

14. Tenayuca and Brooks, 263.

15. Mario Garcia, *Mexican Americans*, 149–151.

16. Allan Turner, "The Night That Changed San Antonio," *Houston Chronicle* December 14th, 1986, 46.

17. "SCHOOL IMPROVEMENT LEAGUE" The Handbook of Texas Online, <http://www.tsha.utexas.edu/handbook/online/articles/view/SS/kaswm.html> [Accessed Saturday January 13th 19:47:10 U.S./Central 2001].

18. Ibid.

19. Maria L. Hernandez, "Programa Litero-Musical Todo en Commemoracíon del 4avo Aniversario de la Orden 'Caballeros de America' October 12, 1969, Harlandale Civic Center, San Antonio, Texas." Vertical File, Benson Latin American Collection, University of Texas at Austin.

20. Hernandez, Maria L. de, *Mexico y Los Cuatro Poderes que Dirigen al Pueblo: la Sociedad, la Politica, el Comercio, la Religion*, (San Antonio: Artes Graphicas, 1945) Rare Book Collection, Benson Latin American Collection, University Of Texas At Austin. Orozco, Cynthia E. "HERNANDEZ, MARIA L. DE," The Handbook of Texas Online, <http://www.tsha.utexas.edu/handbook/online/articles/view/HH/fhe75.html> (Accessed Saturday January 20th 13:52:26 U.S./Central 2001).

21. "SCHOOL IMPROVEMENT LEAGUE"

22. Ibid.

23. Gus C. Garcia, "Address Delivered By Gus C. Garcia at His Testimonial Dinner, February 13th 1952." Escobar Papers, Benson Latin American Collection, University of Texas at Austin.

24. Ibid.

25. "GARCIA, GUSTAVO C." The Handbook Of Texas Online <http://www.tsha.utexas.edu/handbook/online/articles/view/GG/fga51.html> [Accessed Monday January 22 20:05:40 U.S./Central 2001].

26. Ruben Mungia, interview with the author, May 9, 1999 at Mungia Printers, San Antonio Texas. Carlos Cadena, interview with the author May 10, 1999 at the home of the interviewee, San Antonio Texas.

27. *Hernandez v. Texas,* 347 US 475 (1954).
28. Pycior, *LBJ and Mexican Americans,* 202.
29. Richard Garcia, *Rise Of The Middle Class,* 64.
30. Ibid, 208.

NOTES TO CHAPTER FOUR

1. "LULAC Through The Years: History of Former LULAC Presidents," *LULAC News* 21 (8) (February1954), 65.
2. Richard Griswold del Castillo, "Southern California Chicano History: Regional Origins And National Critique" *Aztlan* 19(Spring 1988–90):109.
3. Sanchez, *Becoming Mexican American,* 87–88.
4. Richard Griswold del Castillo, "Tejanos and California Chicanos: Regional Variations in Mexican American History," *Mexican Studies/Estudios Mexicanos* 1(Winter 1985): 138. In the context of Mexican American history, the term Chicano most directly applies to Mexican Americans in California, although it has been used in Texas. This is especially the case since the word became the property of a movement whose intellectual roots are in California.
5. Sanchez, *Becoming Mexican American,* 94–95.
6. Ricardo Romo, *East Los Angeles: History Of A Barrio.* (Austin: University Of Texas Press, 1983), 131–36.
7. Richard Rodriguez, *The Hunger Of Memory* (Boston: David R. Godine, 1981), 124. See also Kevin R. Johnson, *How Did You Get To Be Mexican? A White/Brown Man's Search for Identity,* (Philadelphia: Temple University Press, 1999.
8. Sanchez, *Becoming Mexican American,* 97.
9. Ibid, 105.
10. Allen F. Davis, *Spearheads for Reform: The Social Settlements and the Progressive Movement, 1890–1914,* (London: Oxford University Press, 1967), 89.
11. See Frederick E. Hoxie, *A Final Promise: The Campaign to Assimilate the Indians, 1880–1920.* (Lincoln, Nebraska: University of Nebraska Press, 1984), 15.
12. Sanchez, 104–105.
13. Griswold del Castillo, "Southern California Chicano History," 110.
14. Emory S. Bogardus, "Attitudes and The Mexican Migrant," in *Social Attitudes* ed. Kimball Young [New York: Holt and Co., 1931], 317.
15. Ibid.
16. Carey McWilliams, "Getting Rid of the Mexican," *American Mercury* 28 (March 1933): 324.
17. Sanchez, 214.
18. The intellectual void was parallel to the experience of Japanese Americans immediately after Pearl Harbor. In his study of Nisei identity, David Yoo writes that, "In the process (of incarceration) the government stripped Japanese American communities all along the West Coast of key Issei figures, creating a leadership vacuum that added to mounting confusion and anxiety." David K. Yoo, *Growing Up Nisei: Race, Generations and Culture among Japanese*

Americans of California, 1924–49 (Urbana: University of Illinois Press, 2000), 91.

19. Ibid, 225.
20. Rudolfo Acuña, *Occupied America*, 205.
21. Mauricio Magón, *The Zoot Suit Riots: The Psychology Of Symbolic Annihilation* (Austin: University of Texas Press, 1984), 73.
22. Manuel Gonzales, *Mexicanos*, 170.
23. Sanchez, 274.
24. Griswold del Castillo, "Southern California Chicano History," 110.
25. Sanchez, 88–89.
26. Ibid.
27. Anne Loftis, *Witnesses To The Struggle: Imaging In The 1930's California Labor Movement* (Reno, Nevada: University of Nevada Press, 1998), 19.
28. Loftis, 13.
29. Mario Garcia, *Mexican Americans*, 146–158. Mario Garcia's monograph is the only comprehensive work available on the Congress.
30. Mario Garcia, *Mexican Americans*, 149–150.
31. Ibid, 159–61.
32. Beginning from militant anti-fascism, moving to isolationism after August of 1939, to favoring the Allies after June 1941. Mario Garcia, *Mexican Americans*, 165. The position of the Congress regarding the war revealed that much of the agenda of the Popular Front was directed from the Comintern. See also Loftis, 95.
33. Mario Garcia, *Mexican Americans*, 171.
34. Mario Garcia, *Mexican Americans*, 171–72. See also Manuel P Servín, *The Mexican Americans, An Awakening Minority* [Beverly Hills: Glencoe Press, 1974] for an extensive examination of the Sleepy Lagoon trial and appeal process.
35. Max S. Meier, Introduction to *North from Mexico*, by Carey McWilliams (New York: Praeger, 1990), 15.
36. Loftis, 17, 94.
37. Shirlene Ann Soto, *The Mexican Woman: A Study of Her Participation in the Revolution, 1910–1940*. (Palo Alto, California: R&E Research Associates, 1979), 35 and Loftis, 35.
38. The only intellectual organ in Los Angeles community was the Spanish newspaper *La Opinion* which, like its sister newspaper *La Prensa*, attempted to mold the consciousness of Chicanos in a Mexican direction.

NOTES TO CHAPTER FIVE

1. Raul Morin, *Among the Valiant: Mexican Americans in World War II and Korea*, (Alhambra, Cal.: Bordin, 1966), 24.
2. Richard Garcia, *Rise of the Middle Class*, 303.
3. Karen Brodkin, *How Jews Became White Folks and What That Says about Race in America*, (New Brunswick, NJ: Rutgers University Press, 1998), 141–143.

4. Richard Garcia, "Making of the Mexican American Mind," 124.

5. Barnes, in *Are We Good Neighbors?* 79.

6. Castañeda, in *Are We Good Neighbors?* 20.

7. Saenz, "Racial Discrimination: The Number One Problem in Texas Schools," in *Are We Good Neighbors?* 35.

8. John Frederick Martin, *Civil-Rights and the Crisis of Liberalism: The Democratic Party, 1945–76* (Boulder, Colorado: Westview Press, 1979), 74–75.

9. Alex Avila, "Freedom Fighter," *Hispanic* 9 (January-February 1996):20.

10. Gonzales, *Mexicanos*, 164.

11. Pycior, *LBJ and Mexican Americans*, 60.

12. Ignacio Garcia, *Viva Kennedy*, 73.

13. Henry J. Ramos, *The American G.I. Forum: In Pursuit of The Dream, 1948–1983* (Houston: Arte Publico Press, 1998), 81.

14. Richard Garcia, *Rise of the Mexican American Middle Class*, 313.

15. Castañeda, "Statement on Discrimination Against Mexican-Americans in Employment" in *Are We Good Neighbors?* 59.

16. Saenz in *Are We Good Neighbors?*, 35.

17. Ibid, 33.

18. Ramos, *The American G.I. Forum*, 20.

19. David J. Bogue, *The Population of the United States*, (Glencoe, IL.: Free Press, 1959), 59 in Ignacio Garcia, *United We Win: The Rise and Fall of La Raza Unida Party*, (Tucson: University of Arizona Press, 1989), 172.

20. Acuna, *Occupied America*, 312.

21. Richard Garcia, *Rise of The Middle Class*, 23.

22. Testimony of Rev. Ralph Ruiz, *Hearing U.S. Commission on Civil Rights*, San Antonio, Texas, December 9th–14, 1968 (U.S. G.P.O., 1969), 73.

23. Rodriguez, "Henry B. Gonzalez: A Political Profile," 21.

24. For reasons that will be shown later, the phrase Chicano or Chicana will be used to identify California Mexican Americans, or those who consciously affiliate themselves with the Brown Power movement.

25. Ronnie Dugger, "Gonzalez of San Antonio," part V, "The Politics of Fratricide," *The Texas Observer*, (December 12, 1980), 11.

26. Dugger, "Politics," 15.

27. Dugger, "Gonzalez of San Antonio," part II, "From Revolution to the Capital" *The Texas Observer*, (April 11, 1980), 8.

28. Ibid, 10.

29. My maternal grandfather came to the U.S. under similar circumstances; his father was the owner of a hacienda threatened by the revolution. Eventually, my grandfather made his way to Chicago.

30. Dugger, "From Revolution to the Capital," 20.

31. Ibid.

32. Dugger, "Gonzalez of San Antonio," part III, "The South Texas Cauldron: Guns, Disease, Politics, Victory," *The Texas Observer*, (May 9, 1980), 15, 18.

33. Rodriguez, "Gonzalez," 37–38.

34. Dugger, "The South Texas Cauldron," 15.

35. Rodriguez, "Gonzalez," 51–52.

36. Ibid.

37. Samuel Ramos, *Profile of Man and Culture in Mexico*, (Austin: University of Texas Press, 1962), 57.

38. Ramos, 33.

39. Paz, 10–11.

40. George J. Sanchez, 152.

41. Ibid, 165.

42. Dugger, "The South Texas Cauldron," 18.

43. Thomas Sowell, *Ethnic America: A History* (New York: Basic Books, 1981), 33–34.

44. Dugger, "The South Texas Cauldron," 20.

45. Rodriguez, "Gonzalez," 72.

46. Dugger, "The South Texas Cauldron," 18.

47. Rodriguez, "Gonzalez," 76.

48. *Brown v. Board of Education* 347 U.S. 483 (1954).

49. "History in Texas: A Filibuster AGAINST Jim Crow!" *The Southern Patriot* 15 (May 1957): 1 Henry B. Gonzalez Papers, St. Mary's University Law Library, San Antonio Texas," Texas: For Whom the Bell Tolls," *Time* (May 13, 1957), 27.

50. "For Whom the Bell Tolls."

51. Dugger, "From Revolution to The Capital," 20.

52. Dugger, "The Segregation Filibuster of 1957," *The Texas Observer* 48 (May 7th 1957): 4.

53. Rodriguez, "Gonzalez," 79.

54. Ibid

55. Kemper Diehl, "MAYO Head Warns of Rioting, Violence, " *The Sunday Sun; San Antonio Express-News,* (April 13, 1969), 14 in Eleutrio Escobar Papers, University of Texas at Austin.

56. Diehl, 14.

57. Dugger, "The Politics of Fratricide," 8, 9.

58. Antonio Navarro, *Mexican American Youth Organization: Avant-Garde of The Chicano Movement In Texas* (Austin: University of Texas, 1995), 7.

59. Navarro, 83.

60. Pycior, *LBJ and Mexican Americans*, 206.

61. Navarro, 86.

62. Navarro, 83.

63. John C. Hammerback, Richard J. Jensen and Jose Angel Gutierrez, *A War of Words: Chicano Protest in the 1960s and 1970s* (Westport CT.: Greenwood Press, 1985), 88.

64. Gonzales, *Mexicanos*, 195.

65. Richard Garcia, *Rise of the Middle Class*, 82.

66. Hammerback, 87.

67. Ruben Salazar, *Los Angeles Times*, (February 6, 1970).

68. Hammerback, 156.

69. La Coronela, "Cultural Nationalism: A Fight for Survival," *Chicano Student* 1 (April 25, 1968), 5.

70. Hammerback, 54–55.

71. Pycior, *LBJ and Mexican Americans*, 162.

72. Ignacio Garcia, *United We Win*, 92.

73. Navarro, *MAYO*, 38.

74. Navarro, *MAYO*, 53–54.

75. Hammerback, 92.

76. David J. Weber, *Foreigners in Their Native Land*, 205–06.

77. Hammerback, 57.

78. Manuel Gonzales, *Mexicanos*, 204.

79. Ignacio Garcia, *Chicanismo: The Forging of a Militant Ethos among Mexican-Americans,* (Tucson: University of Arizona Press, 1997), 95.

80. "El Plan Espiritual De Aztlán," in Anaya, Rudolfo and Francisco A. Lomeli. *Aztlán: Essays on the Chicano Homeland.* (Albuquerque, NM: El Norte Publications, 1989), 1, 2.

81. Genero M. Padilla, "Myth and Comparative Cultural Nationalism," in Anaya, *Aztlan*, 112.

82. Tom Tiede, "By Ballot or Bullet, Chicanos out for Equality," *Palo Alto Times* (September 21, 1970), 17.

83. Angie Chabram and Rosa Linda Fregoso, "Chicana/o Cultural Representations: Reframing Alternative Cultural Discourses," *Cultural Studies* 4 (1990): 206 in Daniel Cooper Alarcon, *The Aztec Palimpsest: Mexico in the Modern Imagination,* (Tucson: University of Arizona Press, 1997), 11.

84. Bender, *Intellect and Public Life*, 30–31, see also Thomas L. Haskell, ed., *The Authority of Experts*, (Bloomington, Indiana University Press, 1984).

85. Pycior, *LBJ and Mexican Americans*, 205.

86. Clarence J. La Roche, "Mexican-Americans Given Challenge to up Lot in Life," *San Antonio Express-News*, (January 7, 1968), 1.

87. "The Ghost of Zapata," *San Antonio Express-News*, (January 7, 1968), 10A.

88. Deihl, "Mexican-American Leaders Seek Grass Roots," *San Antonio Express-News,* (January 7, 1968), 1-A. See also Pycior, *LBJ and Mexican Americans*, 205.

89. Henry B. Gonzalez, "Hope and Promise: Americans of Spanish Surname," *American Federationist* (June 1967), 14.

90. Ibid, 15.

91. Gonzalez, "Hope and Promise," 15.

92. Ibid.

93. Robert S. Goizueta, "United States Hispanic Theology and the Challenge of Pluralism" in *Frontiers Of Hispanic Theology in the United States* ed. Allan Figueroa Dech, (Maryknoll, NY: Orbis Books, 1992), 14 in Matovina, 93.

94. Gonzalez, "Hope and Promise," 15.

95. U.S. Congress, House. Congressman Gonzalez, speaking on "The Hate Issue," 91st Cong. 1st sess., *Congressional Record* (April 22, 1969), 9952, 9953.

96. Gonzalez, "The Hate Issue," 9952.

97. Ignacio Garcia, *Viva Kennedy*, 9. One wonders whether the structure of U.S. society has ever allowed for the collective rise of any group, excepting the Puritans of colonial America.

98. David Gonzales, interview with author, Guadalupe Cultural Arts Center, San Antonio, TX, August 13, 2001.

99. Plan de Aztlán.

100. Richard Hofstadter, *Anti-Intellectualism in American Life*, (New York: Knopf, 1963), 418.

101. Richard Garcia, *Rise of the Mexican American Middle Class*, 307.

102. Dugger, "The Politics of Fratricide," 19.

103. Ignacio Garcia, *United We Win*, 202.

NOTES TO THE EPILOGUE

1. Like me, she was born and raised in Chicago, the child of Mexican immigrants.

2. Interview with Sandra Cisneros, October 27, 2001, San Antonio Texas.

3. Garcia, Mario T. "The Chicana in American History: The Mexican Women of El Paso, 1880–1920—A Case Study," *Pacific Historical Review* 49(1980): 315–37.

4. Ginia Bellafonte, "Feminism: It's All about Me!" *Time* (June 29th 1998), 1.

5. Beatriz M. Pesquera and Denise A. Segura, "There Is No Going Back: Chicanas and Feminism," in *Chicana Feminist Thought: The Basic Historical Writings* Alma M. Garcia, ed. (New York: Routledge, 1997), 299.

6. Reyes Rachel Madrigal, "La Chicana and the Movement: Ideology and Identity," Doctoral Dissertation, Clairmont Graduate School, (1977), 16.

7. Pesquera and Segura, "There Is No Going Back," 297.

8. Enriqueta Longeaux y Vasquez, "The Mexican American Woman," in *Readings on La Raza: The Twentieth Century* (New York: Hill and Wang, 1974), 257–258.

9. Anna Nieto Gomez, "Chicana Feminism," in *Chicana Feminist Thought*, 53.

10. Alma Garcia, *Chicana Feminist Thought*, 69.

11. Martha Cotera, *Profile of the Mexican-American Woman*, (Austin: Information Systems Development, 1976), 224.

12. Marta Vidal, "Chicanas Speak Out," in *Chicana Feminist Thought*, 90.

13. See Alma M. Garcia, "The Development of Chicana Feminist Discourse, 1970–1980," 232, and Tey Diana Rebolledo, "Chicana Studies: Is There a Future for Us in Women's Studies?" 36, in Annette Sedillo Lopez, ed. *Latina Issues: Fragments of Historia (ella)(Herstory)*. New York: Garland Publishing, 1995.

14. Sanchez, *Becoming Mexican American*, 8.

15. Cotera, "Keynote Address, Chicana Identity Conference, University of Houston, November 1975," in *Chicana Feminist*, (Austin: Information Systems Development, 1977), 26.

16. Madrigal, "Identity," 17.

17. Sandra Cisneros, *The House on Mango Street*, (New York: Vintage Books, 1991), Back Cover.

18. Cisneros, interview with author.

19. Just a few miles from where I lived as a child.

20. Manuel S. Gonzales, *Mexicanos*, 145.

21. Cisneros, interview with author.

22. Ibid.

23. Cisneros, *The House on Mango Street*, xvi.

24. Cisneros, interview with author.

25. Cisneros, *Woman Hollering Creek, and other Stories*, (New York: Random House, 1991), 61.

26. Cisneros, interview with author.

27. Ruben Mungia, "Three Peas in a Pod," Ruben Mungia Papers, Mungia Printers, San Antonio, Texas, n. p.

28. Cisneros, interview with author.

29. The Virgin of Guadalupe, a vision of a mestiza Virgin Mary, is one of the foundational religious and intellectual symbols of Mexican history.

30. Ibid.

31. Veronica Salazar, *Dedication Rewarded: Prominent Mexican Americans,* (San Antonio, Texas: Mexican American Cultural Center, 1976), 23.

32. Richard Garcia, *Rise of the Mexican American Middle Class,* 321.

33. Beatriz Gallego, interview with the author, April 1999, San Antonio, Texas.

34. Donald C. Bacon, "Close-up of America: San Antonio's Battle to Blend Rival Cultures," *U.S. News and World Report,* (November 24, 1980), 59.

35. Peter Skerry, *Mexican-Americans: An Ambivalent Minority,* (Cambridge, Mass.: Harvard University Press, 1995), 158.

36. Jerry Poyo, Interview with Emma Tenayuca, San Antonio, Texas, February 21, 1987, Institute of Texan Cultures, 19.

37. Gallego, interview with author.

38. Bacon, 58.

39. Salazar, "Henry Cisneros," in *Dedication Rewarded,* 23.

40. Henry Cisneros, "First-Person: The Future of San Antonio," *San Antonio Magazine,* (June 1989), 11.

41. Richard Garcia, *Rise of the Mexican American Middle Class,* 321.

42. David Riesman, *The Lonely Crowd: A Study of the Changing American Character,* (New Haven: Yale University Press, 1950), 257.

43. Pycior, *LBJ and Mexican Americans,* 242.

44. Martin Luther King, Jr. *Stride toward Freedom,* 99, Quoted in Kenneth L. Smith and Ira E. Zipp, Jr. *Search for the Beloved Community: The Thinking of Dr. Martin Luther King, Jr.* (Valley Forge, Penn.: Judson Press, 1974.), 121.

Bibliography

INTERVIEWS

Almaráz, Felix. March 23, 1999, San Antonio, Texas.

Cadena, Carlos. May 10, 1999, San Antonio, Texas.

Cisneros, Sandra. October 2001, San Antonio, Texas.

Gallego, Breatriz. April, 1999, San Antonio, Texas.

Gonzales, David. August 13, 2001. Guadalupe Cultural Arts Center, San Antonio Texas.

Gonzalez, Charles. San Antonio, Texas.

Mugnia, Ruben. San Antonio, Texas.

Poyo, Gerald. Interview with Emma Tenayuca, San Antonio Texas, February 21, 1987. Institute of Texan Cultures.

ARCHIVES

Carlos E. Castañeda Papers. Benson Collection, University of Texas at Austin.

Eleuterio Escobar Papers. Benson Collection, University of Texas at Austin.

Henry B. Gonzalez Papers. St. Mary's University Law Library.

Jose Angel Gutierrez Papers. Benson Collection, University of Texas at Austin.

Ruben Mungia Papers. Mungia Printers, 2201 Buena Vista, San Antonio, Texas.

COURT CASES

Hernandez v. Texas, 347 US 475 (1954).

Independent School District v. Salvatierra, 33 S.W. 2nd 790 (1930).

ARTICLES

Allsup, Carl. "Education is Our Freedom: The American G.I. Forum and the Mexican American School Segregation in Texas, 1948–57." *Aztlán* 8(Spring 1977): 27–50.

Altus, William O. "The American Mexican: The Survival of a Culture." *Journal of Social Psychology* 29 (1949): 218–42.

"A la Prensa, a nuestros amigos y al publico." *La Prensa* February 13, 1913, 1.

Almaguer, Tomás. "Ideological Distortions in Recent Chicano Historiography: The Internal Model and Chicano Historical Interpretation." *Aztlan* 18(1987): 7–28.

Avila, Alex. "Freedom Fighter" *Hispanic* 9(January-February 1996): 18–22.

Bacon, Donald C. "Close-Up of America: San Antonio's Battle to Blend Rival Cultures," *U.S. News and World Report* (November 24, 1980), 58–59.

Bellafonte, Ginia. "Feminism: It's All about Me!" *Time* 151(June 29, 1998): 1–5.

Bongartz, Ron. "The Chicano Rebellion," *Nation,* March 3, 1969.

Burrel, Francisco O. "The Dialogue of Cuco Rocha," *El Grito* 3(Summer 1970): 37–45.

Castaño, Antonio. "Flowers to the Living," *LULAC News* 1(November 1931): 11–14.

Castañeda, Carlos E. "Sor Juana Ines de la Cruz, Primera Feminista de America" *Revista de la Universidad de Mexico* 5(March-April 1933): 365–79.

_____. "Why I Chose History" *The Americas* 8(April 1952): 475–483.

Chabram, Angie and Rosa Linda Fregoso, "Chicana/o Cultural Representation: Reframing Alternative Discourses" *Cultural Studies* 4(1990): 203–12.

Chavez, Linda. "Affirmative Action: A Symposium." *Commentary* 105 (March 1998).

_____. "Our Hispanic Predicament." *Commentary* 105(June 1998): 47–50.

The Chicano Student Movement (Los Angeles), 1968.

Cisneros, Henry. "The Future of San Antonio," *San Antonio Magazine* (June 1989), 11–12.

Cockroft, Eva Sterling. "Chicano Identities" *Art in America* 80(June 92): 84.

Cox, I.J. "Educational Efforts in San Fernando de Bexar," Texas State Historical Association 6(July 1902): 27–63.

Delgado, Fernando Pedro. "Chicano Movement Rhetoric: An Ideographic Interpretation" *Communication Quarterly* 43(Fall 1995): 446–454.

Diehl, Kemper. "MAYO Head Warns of Rioting, Violence." *The Sunday Sun*; *San Antonio Express-News* (April 13, 1969), 14.

_____. "Mexican-American Leaders Seek Grass Roots." *San Antonio Express-News* (January 7, 1968), 1–A, 10–A.

Dugger, Ronnie. "Gonzalez of San Antonio" *The Texas Observer* March 28, April 11, May 9, October 17 and December 12, 1980.

_____. "The Segregation Filibuster of 1957," *The Texas Observer* 48(May 7, 1957): 1, 4.

Dysart, Jane. "Mexican Women in San Antonio, 1830–1860: The Assimilation Process" *Western Historical Quarterly* 7(October 1976): 365–375.

El Grito del Norte. Española, New Mexico, 1968–1973.

Ericksen, Charles A. "Uprising in the Barrios," *American Education* 4(November 1968): 29–31.

Estrada, et al. "Chicanos in the United States: A History of Exploitation and Resistance" *Daedalus* 110(2)(1981): 103–131.

"A 400 Word Start." *Time* August 17, 1957, 56.

Garcia, Ignacio. "La Raza Unida Party, R.I.P." *Nuestro* 4(December 1980): 49.

Garza, Adolf A. "Citizenship," *LULAC News* 1(August 1931): 5.

Garza, George J. "Founding and History of LULAC, League of United Latin American Citizens," *LULAC News* 21 (February 1954): 21–25.

Gleason, Phillip. "Identifying Identity: A Semantic History," *Journal of American History* 69 (March 1983): 910–931.

Gonzales, M.C. "Echoes of the Kingsville Convention," *LULAC News* 1(September 1931): 7–8.

Gonzalez, Alberto. "Mexican 'Otherness' in the Rhetoric of Mexican Americans." *Southern Communication Journal* 55(Spring 1990): 276.

Gonzalez, Henry B. "Hope and Promise: Americans of Spanish Surname," *American Federationist* June 1967.

_____. "The Mexican-American: An Awakening Giant," *Employment Service Review,* July 1967.

Grandjeat, Yves-Charles. "Conflicts and Cohesiveness: The Elusive Quest for a Chicano History." *Aztlan* 18(Spring 1987): 45.

Granneberg, Audrey. "Maury Maverick's San Antonio" *Survey Graphic* 1, no. 28 (1939): 423–30.

Handlin, Oscar and Mary Handlin. "The New History and Ethnic Factor in American Life." *Perspectives on American History* 4 (1970): 5–24.

Handman, Max S. "San Antonio: The Old Capital City of Mexican Life and Influence." *Survey Graphic* 66 (1931): 160–68.

Hazuda, Helen P., Stern, Michael P. and Steven M. Haffner, "Acculturation and Assimilation among Mexican Americans: Scales and Population-Based Data," *Social Science Quarterly* 69(3)(1988): 687–706.

"Henry B. Gonzalez: 30 Years on the Hill," *Austin American-Statesman,* November 4, 1991.

Hernández, Francisco. "Mexican Gender Studies and the American University." *American Behavioral Scientist* 40 (June/July 1997): 968–974.

Hernandez, Maria L. Programa Litero-Musical Todo en Commemeración del 4avo. Aniversario de la Orden "Caballeros de America" 12 October 1969,

Harlandale Civic Center, San Antonio, Texas. Vertical File, Benson Latin American Collection, University of Texas at Austin.

"History in Texas: A Filibuster AGAINST Jim Crow!" *The Southern Patriot* 15(May 1957): 1, 2.

Holler, Stephen C. "Exploring the Popular Religion of U.S. Hispanic/Latino Ethnic Groups," *Latino Studies Journal* 6(3)(1995): 3–29.

Hurtado, Aída and Carlos H. Arce. "Mexicans, Chicanos, Americans or Pochos...?Que somos? The Impact of Language and Nativity on Ethnic Labeling." *Aztlan* 17 (1986): 103–130.

Ibañez, Manuel Ruiz. "Spanish-Language Press Had a Vital Role in San Antonio History," *San Antonio Express*, (June 18, 1972).

Jones, O. "Hispanic Traditions and Improvisations" *New Mexico Historical Review* 56(4)(1981): 333–47.

Jones, Robert C. "Ethnic Family Patterns: The Mexican Family in the United States" *American Journal of Psychology* 53 (1948): 450–53.

Jordan, Terry. "A Century and a Half of Ethnic Change in Texas, 1836–1986" *Southwest Historical Quarterly* 89(April 1986): 400.

Kaup, Monika. "The Architecture of Ethnicity in Chicano Literature" *American Literature* 69 (June 1997): 361–397.

La Prensa. San Antonio, Texas (1913–1963).

Lejeune, Catherine. "The Challenge Facing America over the Chicano Identity Question in Light of the Quincentenary Celebration of 1992" *North Dakota Quarterly* 60(1)(1992): 174–79.

Lessoff, Alan. "A Texas City and the Texas Myth" *Southwestern Historical Quarterly* 100(January 1997): 300.

Longeaux y Vasquez, Enriqueta. "Soy Chicana Primero" *La Raza Habla* 1(January 1976): 1–5.

"LULAC through the Years: History of Former LULAC Presidents," *LULAC News* 21(February 1954): 65–75.

Madrid Barela, Arturo. "Towards an Understanding of the Chicano Experience" *Aztlan* 4(1)(1973): 185–93.

Maitlan, Ralph. "San Antonio, The Shame of Texas." *Forum and Century* 102 (1939): 50–54.

Manuel, H.T. "Education of Mexican and Spanish-speaking Children in Texas," In *Education and the Mexican American,* ed. Carlos Cortez, New York: Arno Press, 1974.

————. "Education, the Guardian of Democracy and the Hope of the Youth," *LULAC News* 7 no. 3(November 1940): 1.

————. "The Mexican Population in Texas," *Southwestern Social Science Quarterly* 15 (1934):29–51.

Marquez, Benjamin. "The Politics of Race and Class: The League of United Latin American Citizens in the Post World War II Period." *Social Science Quarterly* 68, no. 1 (March 1987): 84–101.

Matovina, Timothy M. "Religion and Ethnicity in San Antonio: Germans and Tejanos in the Wake of United States Annexation." *Catholic Southwest.* 29–49.

McCrory, Jim. "What Makes Henry B. Run?" *San Antonio News* (January 6–10, 1974).

McLemore, S. Dale. "The Origins of Mexican American Subordination in Texas," *Social Science Quarterly* 53(March 1973)656–671.

McWilliams, Carey. "Getting Rid of the Mexican," *American Mercury* 28(March 1933): 322–24.

Muñoz, Carlos. "Making of the Chicano Movement Revisited" *Black Issues in Higher Education* 13(April 4, 1996): 72.

Navarro, Armando. "The Evolution of Chicano Politics." *Aztlan* 5(Spring 1974): 57–84.

Norstrand, Richard L. "'Mexican-American' and 'Chicano'" *Pacific Historical Review* 42(3)(1973): 389–406.

Orozco, Cynthia E. "Beyond Machismo, La Familia, and Ladies' Auxiliaries: A Historiography of Mexican-Origin Women's Participation in Voluntary Associations and Politics in the United States, 1870–1990." *Perspectives in Mexican American Studies* 5(1995): 3–34.

Parades, Raymond A. "The Origins of Anti-Mexican Sentiment in the United States" *New Scholar* 6(1977): 158.

Parra, Ricardo. "Chicano Organizations in the Midwest: Past, Present and Possibilities," *Aztlan* 7(2)(1976): 235–253.

Peña, Richard. "Will the Real Chicano Please Stand Up?" *Magazin* 1(December 1971): 9–13.

Perales, Alonzo S. "La Evolucion de la Raza Mexicana," *La Prensa* September 13, 1927, 1,9.

_____. "La Unificacíon de los Mexico Americanos," *La Prensa* September 4, 1929, 1,5.

Pinedo, Frank. "A Life That's Worth Living." *LULAC News* 21(February 1954): 43–44.

Poulos, William T. "They Learn Basic English before School Starts," *Texas Outlook* 43(August 1958): 15–34.

Quintana, Helena. "Review of *Viva La Raza: The Struggle of the Mexican-American People*" *De Colores* 2 (1975): 74–75.

Romo, Ricardo. "George I. Sanchez and the Civil Rights Movement: 1940–1960" *La Raza Law Journal* 1(1986): 343–362.

Saenz, J. Luz. "Has the Time Come?" *Texas Outlook* 26 (April 1942): 44.

Saenz, Rogelio. "The Dynamics of Mexican-American Ethnic Identity" *Ethnic Groups* 9(February 1991): 17.

Sanchez, George I. "The American of Mexican Descent" *The Chicago Jewish Forum* 20(Winter 1961–62): 120–24.

_____. "Bilingualism and Mental Measures: A Word of Caution" *Journal of Applied Psychology* 8(December 1934): 765–772.

————. "Spanish Name Spells Discrimination" *Nation's Schools* 41 (January 1948): 22–24.

Sierra, Christine Marie. "Mexicans in the United States: History, Evolution and Transformation" *Latin American Research Review* 24(Spring 1989): 218.

Skerry, Peter. "Neighborhood COPS: The Resurrection of Saul Alinsky," *New Republic* (February 6, 1984), 21–23.

Slobada, Nicholas. "A Home in the Heart: Sandra Cisneros' *House on Mango Street*" *Aztlan* 22(Fall 1997): 89–105.

Stilwell, Hart. "Texas Rebel with a Cause," *Coronet* August 1958, 43–47.

Stoltz, Alberta and H.T. Manuel. "Art Ability of Mexican Children," *School and Society* 34 (September 12, 1931): 379–380.

Tenayuca, Emma and Homer Brooks. "The Mexican Question in the Southwest" *The Communist* (March 1939): 257–268.

"Texas: For Whom the Bell Tolls." *Time* (May 13, 1957), 27.

Treviño, Roberto R. *"Prensa y Patria:* The Spanish-Language Press and the Biculturation of the Middle Class, 1920–1940" *Western Historical Quarterly* 22(November 1991): 451–74.

Turner, Allan. "A Night that Changed San Antonio." *Houston Chronicle* December 14, 1986, 1, 46.

U.S. Congress. House. Representative Henry B. Gonzalez, Speech, 91st Cong., 1st sess. *Congressional Record* (April 22, 1969), 9951–9954.

Vaca, Nick C., Octavio I. Romano and Andres Ybarra, eds. *El Grito: A Journal of Contemporary Mexican Thought.* Berkeley: Quinto Del Sol, Vols. 1–7, 1967–73.

Zamora, Emilio, Jr. "Chicano Socialist Labor Activity in Texas, 1900–1920," *Aztlan* 6(Summer 1975): 221–38.

BOOKS

Acuña, Rudolfo. *A Community under Siege: A Chronicle of Chicanos East of the Los Angeles River, 1945–75.* Los Angeles: Chicano Studies Research Center Publications, University of California at Los Angeles, 1984.

————. *Occupied America: A History of Chicanos.* New York: Harper and Row, 1981.

Alarcón, Daniel Cooper. *The Aztec Palimpsest: Mexico in the Modern Imagination.* Tucson: University of Arizona Press, 1990.

Allsup, Carl. *The American G.I. Forum: Origins and Evolution.* Austin: University of Texas Press, 1982.

Almaraz, Felix D. *Knight without Armor: Carlos Eduardo Castañeda, 1896–1958.* College Station: Texas A&M University Press, 1999.

Alonzo, Armando C. *Tejano Legacy: Rancheros and Settlers in South Texas, 1734–1900.* Albuquerque: University of New Mexico Press, 1998.

Alva Ixtlilxochitl, Fernando de. *Ally of Cortes.* Trans. Douglas K. Ballentine. El Paso, Texas: Texas Western Press, 1969.

Anaya, Rudolfo and Francisco A. Lomeli. *Aztlan: Essays on the Chicano Homeland.* Albuquerque, N.M.: El Norte Publications, 1989.

Anzaldua, Gloria. *Borderlands/La Frontera: The New Mestiza.* San Francisco: Spinsters/Aunt Lute, 1987.

Bailyn, Bernard. *The Ideological Origins of the American Revolution.* Cambridge: Belknap Press, 1967.

Barker, E. Shannon. "Los Tejanos in San Antonio: Mexican Immigrant Family Acculturation, 1880–1929." Doctoral Dissertation, George Washington University, 1996.

Barrera, Mario. *Beyond Aztlan: Ethnic Autonomy in Comparative Perspective.* New York: Praeger, 1988.

_____. *Race and Class in the Southwest: A Theory of Racial Inequality.* Notre Dame, Indiana: Notre Dame University Press, 1979.

_____. *Work, Family, Sex Roles, and Language.* Berkeley: Tonatiuh-Quinto Sol International, 1980.

Bedillo, David A. *From West San Antonio to East L.A.: Chicano Community Leadership Compared.* Stanford: Stanford University Press, 1989.

Beezley, William. "San Antonio: Capital of Insurgent Mexico." In ed. Howard L. Korso, 43–51. Albuquerque: Seminar on the Acquisition of Latin American Library Materials, 1993.

Bennett, William J. *The Devaluing of America: The Fight for Our Culture and Our Children.* New York: Touchstone, 1992.

Bierhorst, John, trans. *History and Mythology of the Aztecs: The Codex Chimalpopoca.* Tucson: University of Arizona Press, 1992.

Biography of Hector P. Garcia, Founder, American G.I. Forum of the United States. n.p. (American G.I. Forum Archives).

Blackwelder, Julia Kirk. *Women of the Depression: Caste and Culture in San Antonio, 1929–39.* College Station: Texas A&M University Press, 1984.

Blauner, Robert. *Racial Oppression in America.* New York: Harper and Row, 1972.

Brischetto, Robert R. *Chicano Social Movements: A Bibliography.* Austin: University of Texas Press, 1971.

Bogardus, Emory S. "Attitudes and the Mexican Immigrant." In *Social Attitudes* ed. Kimball Young, New York: Henry Holt, 1931.

Brodkin, Karen. *How Jews Became White Folks and What That Says about Race in America.* New Brunswick, NJ: Rutgers University Press, 1998.

Brook, Robert C. "One of the Four Hundred and Thirty-Four: Maury Maverick of Texas." In *The American Politician,* ed. J.T. Salter. Raliegh: University Of North Carolina Press, 1938.

Broyles-Gonzalez, Yolanda *El Teatro Campesino: Theater in the Chicano Movement.* Austin: University of Texas Press, 1994.

Buck, Samuel M. *Yanaguana's Successors: The Story of the Canary Islander's Immigration to Texas in the Eighteenth Century.* San Antonio: Naylor, 1949.

Burkhart, Louise M. *The Slippery Earth: Nahua-Christian Moral Dialogue in Sixteenth-Century Mexico*. Tucson, Arizona: University of Arizona Press, 1989.

Busto, Rudy Val. "Like A Mighty Rushing Wind: The Religious Impulse in the Life and Writing of Reies Lopez Tijerina" Doctoral Dissertation, University of California at Berkeley, 1991.

Cabello-Argandona, Roberto. *The Chicana: A Comprehensive Bibliographic Essay*. Los Angeles, 1975.

Callcott, Willfrid Hardy. *Church and State in Mexico, 1822–1857*. New York: Octagon Books, 1971.

Canales, Jose Thomas, ed. *Bits of Texas History, The Melting Pot of America*. San Antonio: Artes Graficas, 1950.

Carey-Herrera, Patrick. *Chicanismo: Seven Essays Concerning Chicano Thought and Behavior*. Torrence, Calif., Martin Press, 1983.

Carranza, Elihu. *Chicanismo: Philosophical Fragments*. Dubuque, Iowa, Kendall/Hunt, 1978.

Castañeda, Carlos E. *Our Catholic Heritage in Texas, 1519–1936*. Vol. 7, *The Church in Texas Since Independence, 1836–1950*. Austin: von Boeckmann-Jones Company, 1958.

Chavez, Linda. *Out of the Barrio: Toward a New Politics of Cultural Assimilation*. New York: Basic Books, 1991.

Cisneros, Sandra. *The House on Mango Street*. New York, Alfred A. Knopf, 1995.

_____. *Woman Hollering Creek and Other Stories*. New York: Vintage Books, 1991.

Corwin, Arthur F., ed. *Immigrants-and Immigrants*. Westport, Conn., Greenwood Press, 1978.

Cotera, Marta. *The Chicana Feminist*. Austin: Informations Systems Development, 1977.

_____. *The Profile of the Mexican American Woman*. Austin: Information Systems Development, 1976.

Croly, Herbert. *The Promise of American Life*. New York: Macmillan, 1909.

Cruz, Gilberto Rafael. *Let There Be Towns: Spanish Municipal Origins in Mexico and the Southwest*. College Station: Texas A&M University Press, 1998.

Davalos, Karen Mary. "Ethnic Identity among Mexican and Mexican American Women in Chicago, 1920–1991." Ph.D. thesis, Yale University, 1993.

Davis, Allen F. *Spearheads for Reform: The Social Settlements and the Progressive Movement, 1890–1914*. London: Oxford University Press, 1967.

Davis, Marilyn P. *Mexican Voices/American Dreams: An Oral History of Mexican Immigration to the United States*. New York: Henry Holt, 1990.

de la Cruz, Juana Inés. *A Woman of Genius: The Intellectual Autobiography of Juana Inés de la Cruz*. trans. Margaret Sayers Peden. Salisbury, Conn.: Lime Rock Press, 1982.

de las Casas, Bartolome. *A Very Brief Account of the Destruction of the Indies*. 1552.

de la Garza, Rodolfo O. *The Impact of Mexican Immigrants on the Political Behavior of Chicanos.* Austin, Texas: University of Texas, 1983.

_____. *Texas Hispanic Perspectives.* Claremont, Cal.: Tomás Rivera Center, 1996.

_____. *Will the Real Americans Please Stand Up: Anglo and Mexican Support of Core American Political Values.* Austin: University of Texas at Austin, 1995.

de la Teja, Jesus. *San Antonio: A City on New Spain's Far Northern Frontier.* Albuquerque: University of New Mexico Press, 1995.

De Leon, Arnoldo. *The Tejano Community, 1836–1900.* Albuquerque: University of New Mexico Press, 1982.

_____. *They Called Them Greasers: Anglo Attitudes toward Mexicans in Texas, 1821–1900.* Austin: University of Texas Press, 1983.

_____. "White Racial Attitudes toward Mexicanos in Texas, 1821–1900" Doctoral Dissertation, Texas Christian University, 1974.

Dickey, Dan William. *The Kennedy Corridos: A Study of the Ballads of a Mexican American Hero.* Austin: University of Texas, 1978.

diStephano, Onofre. "*La Prensa* of San Antonio and its Literary Page, 1913–1915." Doctoral Dissertation, University of California at Los Angeles, 1983.

Earle, Robert L. and John D. Wirth, eds. *Identities in North America: The Search for Community.* Stanford: Stanford University Press, 1995.

Everett, Donald E. *San Antonio Legacy.* San Antonio: Trinity University Press, 1979.

Federal Writers Project, Works Progress Administration, American Guide Series. *San Antonio: An Authoritative Guide to the City and its Environs.* San Antonio: The Clegg Co., 1938.

Foley, Douglas E. *From Peones to Politicos: Class and Ethnicity in a South Texas Town, 1900–1987.* Austin: University of Texas Press, 1988.

Fowler-Solomini, Heather and Mary Kay Vaughn, eds. *Women of the Mexican Countryside 1850–1990.* Tucson: University of Arizona Press, 1994.

French, Warren, ed. *Chicano Literature.* Boston: Twayne Publishers, 1982.

Garcia, Alma M., ed. *Chicana Feminist Thought: The Basic Historical Writings.* New York: Routledge, 1997.

García, Gustavo. "Address Delivered by Gus C. García at his Testimonial Dinner, February 13, 1952 San Antonio, Texas, Casa Blanca Restaurant" Escobar Papers, Benson Collection, University of Texas at Austin.

Garcia, Ignacio M. *Chicanismo: The Forging of Militant Ethos among Mexican Americans.* Tucson, Ariz., University of Arizona Press, 1997.

_____. *United We Win: The Rise and Fall of the La Raza Unida Party.* Tucson: University of Arizona, 1989.

_____. *Viva Kennedy: Mexican Americans in Search of Camelot.* College Station: Texas A&M University Press, 2000.

Garcia, Mario T. *Mexican Americans: Leadership, Ideology and Identity, 1930–1960.* New Haven: Yale University Press, 1989.

_____. Memories of Chicano History: The Life and Narrative of Bert Corona. Berkeley: University of California Press, 1994.

_____. and Francisco Lomelí, eds. History, Culture and Society: Chicano Studies in the 1980s. Ypsilanti: Bilingual Review Press, 1983.

Garcia, Richard A. "The Making of the Mexican-American Mind, San Antonio, Texas, 1929–1940" Ph.D. Dissertation, University of California, Irvine, 1980.

_____. Rise of the Mexican American Middle Class, San Antonio, 1929–41. Forward by Henry C. Schmidt. College Station: Texas A&M University Press, 1991.

Garcia-Marquez, Gabriel. One Hundred Years of Solitude. trans. Gregory Rabassa. New York: Harper and Row, 1970.

Geue, Chester and Ethel W. A New Land Beckoned: German Immigration to Texas, 1844–1847. Waco, Texas: Texian Press, 1972.

Gish, Theodore and Richard Spuler, eds. Eagle in the New World: German Immigration to Texas and America. College Station: Texas A&M University Press, 1986.

Glazer, Nathan and Daniel P. Moynihan. Ethnicity, Theory and Experience. Cambridge: Harvard University Press, 1975.

Gómez-Quiñones, Juan. Chicano Politics: Reality and Promise, 1940–1990. Albuquerque: University of New Mexico Press, 1990.

_____. Roots of Chicano Politics, 1600–1940. Albuquerque: University of New Mexico Press, 1994.

Gonzales, Manuel G. Mexicanos: a History of Mexicans in the United States. Bloomington: Indiana University Press, 1999.

Gonzales, Sylvia A. 'La Chicana' in Comparative Perspectives of Third World Women. New York: Praeger, 1980.

Gonzalez, Rodolfo. I Am Joaquin: An Epic Poem. n.p., 1967.

Gorodezky, Sylvia. Arte Chicano como Cultura de Protesta. Mexico City: Universidad Nacional Autónoma de México, 1993.

Griswold del Castillo, Richard. La Familia: Chicano Families in the Urban Southwest: 1848 to the Present. Notre Dame, Ind.: University of Notre Dame Press, 1984.

Gutierrez, David. Between Two Worlds: Mexican Immigrants in the United States. Wilmington, Del.: Scholarly Resources, 1996.

_____. CASA in the Chicano Movement: Ideology and Organizational Politics in the Chicano Community. Palo Alto, Cal.: Stanford University Press, 1984.

_____. Ethnicity, Ideology, and Political Development Mexican Immigration as a Political Issue in the Chicano Community, 1910–the Present. 1988.

_____. Walls and Mirrors: Mexican Americans, Mexican Immigrants and the Politics of Ethnicity. Berkeley: University of California Press, 1995.

Hammerback, John C., Richard J. Jensen, and Jose Angel Gutierrez. A War of Words: Chicano Protest in the 1960s and 1970s. Westport Conn.: Greenwood Press, 1985.

Handlin, Oscar. *The Uprooted: The Epic Story of the Great Migrations that Made the American People.* Boston: Little and Brown, 1951.

Hanke, Lewis. *Bartolome De Las Casas: Bookman, Scholar and Propagandist.* Philadelphia: University of Philadelphia Press, 1952.

Hansen, Marcus Lee, "The Problem of the Third Generation Immigrant." Rock Island: Swenson Swedish Immigration Research Center, 1987.

Herberg, Will. *Protestant-Catholic-Jew: An Essay in American Religious Sociology.* Garden City, NY: Anchor, 1960.

Hernandez, Jose Amaro. *Mutual Aid For Survival: The Case Of The Mexican American.* Malabar, Florida: Krieger, 1983.

Herrera-Sobek, Maria. "The Function of Folklore in Gabriel Garcia Marquez." Doctoral Dissertation, University of California at Los Angeles, 1975.

_____. and Helena María Viramontes, eds. *Chicana Creativity and Criticism: Charting New Frontiers in American Literature.* Houston, Tex.: Arte Publico Press, 1988.

Hinojosa, Fredrico Allen. *El Mexico de Afuera.* San Antonio: Artes Graficas, 1940.

Hofstadter, Richard. *Anti-Intellectualism in American Life.* New York: Knopf, 1963.

Hollinger, David A. *In the American Province: Studying the History and the Historiography of Ideas.* Bloomington, Indiana: Indiana University Press, 1985.

Hoxie, Frederick E. *A Final Promise: The Campaign to Assimilate the Indians, 1880–1920.* Lincoln: University of Nebraska Press, 1984.

Johnson, Kevin. *"How Did You Get to Be Mexican?" A White/Brown Man's Search for Identity.* Philadelphia: Temple University Press, 1999.

Jumonville, Neil. *Critical Crossings: The New York Intellectuals in Postwar America.* Berkeley: University of California Press, 1991.

Keen, Benjamin. *The Aztec Image in Western Thought.* New Brunswick, N.J.: Rutgers University Press, 1990.

Kibbe, Pauline R. *Latin Americans in Texas.* Albuquerque: University of New Mexico Press, 1946.

Kivisto, Peter and Dag Blanck. *American Immigrants and their Generations: Studies and Commentaries on the Hansen Thesis after Fifty Years.* Chicago: University of Illinois Press, 1990.

Koestler, Arthur. *The God that Failed.* Edited by Richard Crossman. New York: Harper and Brothers, 1949.

León-Portilla, Miguel. *Aztec Thought and Culture: A Study of the Ancient Nahuatl Mind.* trans. Jack Emory Davis. Norman: University of Oklahoma Press, 1969.

Lich, Glen E. *The German Texans.* San Antonio: Institute of Texan Cultures, 1981.

Loftis, Anne. *Witness to the Struggle: Imaging The 1930's California Labor Movement.* Reno: University of Nevada Press, 1998.

Lopez, Annette Sedillo, ed. *Latina Issues: Fragments of Historia (ella) (Herstory).* New York: Garland Publishing, 1995.

López, Tiffany Ana, ed. *Growing up Chicana/o: An Anthology*. New York: William and Morrow, 1993.

Lowrie, Samuel Harmon. *Culture Conflict in Texas, 1821–1835*. New York: AMS Press, 1967.

Ludwig, Ed and James Santibanez, eds. *The Chicanos: Mexican American Voices*. Baltimore: Penguin, 1971.

LULAC. *What Price Education? 1962 Report on the Little School of 400*. Austin: LULAC Educational Fund, 1962. (Guadalupe Quintanilla Files).

Maciel, David and Isidoro D. Ortiz, eds. *Chicanos/Chicanas at the Crossroads: Social Economic and Political Change*. Tucson: University of Arizona Press, 1996.

Madrigal, Reyes Rachel, "La Chicana and the Movement: Ideology and Identity," Ph.D. Dissertation, Claremont Graduate School (1977).

Magón, Mauricio. *The Zoot Suit Riots: The Psychology of Symbolic Annihilation*. Austin: University Of Texas Press, 1984.

Manefee, Seldon C. and Orin C. Cassmore. *Pecan Shellers: The Problem of Underpaid and Unemployed Mexican Labor*. Washington, D.C. GPO, 1940.

Marquez, Benjamin. *LULAC: Evolution of a Mexican American Political Organization*. Austin: University of Texas Press, 1993.

Martin, John Frederick. *Civil-rights and the Crisis of Liberalism: The Democratic Party, 1945–76*. Boulder, Colorado: Westview Press, 1979.

Matovina, Timothy. *Tejano Religion and Ethnicity: San Antonio, 1821–1860*. Austin: University of Texas Press, 1995.

McWilliams, Carey. *North from Mexico: The Spanish-speaking People of the United States*. New York: J.B. Lippincott Co., 1949.

Meier, Matt S., comp. *Bibliography of Mexican American History*. Westport, Conn.: Greenwood Press, 1984.

————. and Feliciano Rivera, eds. *Readings on La Raza: The Twentieth Century*. New York: Hill and Wang, 1974.

Mexican Americans: Are They an Ambivalent Minority? Claremont, Cal.: Tomás Rivera Center, 1994.

Meyer, Doris. *Speaking for Themselves: Neomexicano Cultural Identity and the Spanish-language Press, 1880–1920*. Albuquerque: University of New Mexico Press, 1996.

Miller, Perry. *Errand into the Wilderness*. Cambridge Mass.: Belknap Press, 1956.

Mirandé, Alfredo. *The Chicano Experience: An Alternative Perspective*. Notre Dame: University of Notre Dame Press, 1985.

————. and Evangelina Enriquez. *La Chicana: The Mexican-American Woman*. Chicago: University of Chicago Press, 1979.

Montejano, David. *Anglos and Mexicans in the Making of Texas, 1836–1986*. Austin: University of Texas Press, 1987.

Morin, Raúl. *Among the Valiant: Mexican Americans in World War II and Korea*. Alhambra, Cal.: Bordin, 1966.

Muñoz, Carlos Jr. *Youth, Identity, and Power: The Chicano Movement*. London: Verso, 1989.

Mungia, Ruben. *La Prensa*. San Antonio, Texas: Universidad Nacional de Mexico, 1987.

Murgia, Edward. *Assimilation, Colonialism, and the Mexican American People*. Austin: University of Texas, 1975.

Nabokov, Peter. *Tijerina and the Courthouse Raid*. Albuquerque: University of New Mexico Press, 1969.

Navarro, Armando. *Mexican American Youth Organization: Avant-Garde of the Chicano Movement in Texas*. Austin: University of Texas Press, 1995.

Olmstead, Frederick Law. *A Journey Through Texas or, A Saddle-trip on the Southwestern Frontier*. New York: Dix, Edwards and Co., 1857.

Orozco, Cynthia E. "The Origins of the League of United Latin American Citizens (LULAC) and the Mexican American Civil Rights Movement in Texas with an Analysis of Women's Political Participation in a Gendered Context," Ph.D. Dissertation, University of California at Los Angeles, 1992.

Paredes, Americo. *With a Pistol in His Hand: A Border Ballad and Its Hero*. Austin: University of Texas Press, 1958.

_____. and Raymond Paredes, eds. *Mexican American Authors*. Boston: Houghton Mifflin, 1972.

Paredes, Raymond and Ricardo Romo, eds. *New Directions in Chicano Scholarship*. La Jolla, Cal.: University of California at San Diego, 1978.

Pareles, Alonso. *Are We Good Neighbors?* San Antonio: Artes Graficas, 1948.

_____. *En Defensa de Mi Raza*. 2 Vols. San Antonio: Artes Graficas, 1937.

Paz, Octavio, *The Labyrinth of Solitude; Life and Thought in Mexico*. New York: Grove Press, 1961.

Perez-Torres, Rafael. *Movements in Chicano Poetry: Against Myths, against Margins*. New York: Cambridge University Press, 1995.

Poyo, Gerald E. and Gilberto M. Hinojosa, eds. *Tejano Origins in Eighteenth-Century San Antonio*. Austin: University of Texas Press, 1991.

Pycior, Julie Leininger. *LBJ and Mexican Americans: The Paradox of Power*. Austin: University of Texas Press, 1997.

Ramos, Henry. *The American GI Forum: In Pursuit of a Dream, 1948–1983*. Houston: Arte Publico Press, 1998.

Ramos, Samuel. *Profile of Man and Culture in Mexico*. Austin: University of Texas Press, 1962.

Rendon, Armando. "La Raza-Today Not Mañana" in *Mexicans in the United States: A Reader*, ed. John Burma, Cambridge Mass.: Schenkman, 1970.

Ricard, Robert. *The Spiritual Conquest of Mexico: An Essay on the Apostolate and the Evangelizing Methods of the Mendicant Orders in New Spain, 1523–1572*. Berkeley: University of California Press, 1966.

Riesman, David. *The Lonely Crowd: A Study of the Changing American Character*. New Haven, Yale University Press, 1950.

Rochlin, Jay M. *Race and Class on Campus: Conversations with Ricardo's Daughter.* Tucson: University of Arizona Press, 1997.

Rodriguez, Eugene. "Henry B. Gonzalez: A Political Profile." Master's Thesis, St. Mary's University (May, 1965).

Rodriguez, Richard. *Hunger of Memory.* Boston: David R. Godine, 1981.

Rodriguez, Roberto. *The Origins and History of the Chicano Movement.* East Lansing, Mich.: Julian Samora Research Institute, Michigan State University, 1996.

Rogers, Mary Beth. *Cold Anger: A Story of Faith and Power Politics.* Denton: University of North Texas Press, 1990.

Romo, Ricardo. *East Los Angeles: The History of a Barrio.* Austin: University of Texas Press, 1983.

Rosales, F. Arturo. *Chicano! The History of the Mexican American Civil Rights Movement.* Houston: Arte Publico Press, 1996.

Ruiz, Vicki L. and Ellen Carol Du Bois. *Unequal Sisters: A Multicultural Reader in U.S. Women's History.* 3rd ed. New York: Routledge, 2000.

Sahagún, Bernardino de, *Historia General de las Cosas de Nueva España.* (General History of the Things of New Spain); Florentine Codex. Santa Fe, New Mexico, School of American Research, 1975.

Salazar, Veronica. *Dedication Rewarded: Prominent Mexican Americans.* San Antonio, Texas: Mexican American Cultural Center, 1976.

Samora, Julian. *History of the Mexican American People.* Notre Dame, Ind.: University of Notre Dame Press, 1993.

_____. *Los Mojados: The Wetback Story.* Notre Dame, Ind.: University of Notre Dame Press, 1971.

_____. *Minority Leadership in a Bi-cultural Community.* San Francisco: R and E Research Associates, 1973.

San Miguel, Guadalupe. *"Let All of Them Take Heed:" Mexican Americans and the Campaign for Educational Equality in Texas, 1910–1981.* Austin: University of Texas Press, 1987.

Sanchez, George I. *Concerning Segregation of Spanish-Speaking Children in the Public Schools.* Inter-American Occasional Papers no. 9 Austin: University of Texas Press, 1951.

_____. "History, Culture and Education" in *La Raza: The Forgotten Americans* ed. Julian Samora. Notre Dame, Ind.: University of Notre Dame Press, 1966.

Sanchez, George J. *Becoming Mexican American: Ethnicity, Culture and Identity in Chicano Los Angeles, 1900–1945.* New York: Oxford University Press, 1993.

Sanchez, Trinidad. *Why Am I So Brown?* Chicago: Abrazo Press, 1991.

Servín, Manuel P. *The Mexican-Americans: An Awakening Minority.* Beverly Hills, Glencoe Press, 1970.

Shockley, John Staples. *Chicano Revolt in a Texas Town.* Notre Dame, Ind.: Notre Dame University Press, 1974.

Skerry, Peter. *Mexican Americans: The Ambivalent Minority.* Cambridge, Mass: Harvard University Press, 1995.

Sloss-Vento, Adela. *Alonso S. Perales: His Struggle for the Rights of Mexican Americans.* Introduction by Arnold C. Vento. San Antonio: Artes Graficas, 1977.

Smith, Kenneth L. and Ira E. Zipp, Jr. *Search for the Beloved Community: The Thinking of Dr. Martin Luther King, Jr.* Valley Forge, Penn.: Judson Press, 1974.

Soto, Shirlene Ann. *The Mexican Woman: A Study of Her Participation in the Revolution, 1910–1940,* Palo Alto, California, R&E Research Associates, 1979.

Spicer, Edward H. and Raymond H. Thompson, eds. *Plural Society in the Southwest.* New York: Interbook, 1972.

Suro, Roberto. *Strangers among Us: How Latino Immigration is Transforming America.* New York: Alfred Knopf, 1998.

Takaki, Ronald. *From Different Shores: Perspectives on Race and Ethnicity.* New York: Oxford University Press, 1994.

Tavard, George H. *Juana Ines de la Cruz and the Theology of Beauty: The First Mexican Theology.* Notre Dame: University of Notre Dame Press, 1991.

Taylor, Paul S. *Mexican Labor in the United States: Dimmit County, Winter Garden District, South Texas.* Chapel Hill: University of North Carolina Press, 1934.

Tijerina, Reies Lopez. *Mi Lucha por Mi Tierra.* Mexico: Funda de Cultura Economica, 1978.

de Tocqueville, Alexis. *Democracy in America.* ed. J.P. Mayer. New York: Harper Perennial, 1988.

Turkel, Studs. *Coming of Age: The Story of Our Century by Those Who've Lived It.* New York: Norton, 1995.

United States Civil Rights Commission. Hearing before United States Commission on Civil Rights, San Antonio, Texas, December 9–14, 1968. Washington, D.C.: GPO, 1969.

Valdez, Luis and Stanley Steiner, comps. *Aztlan: An Anthology of Mexican American Literature.* New York: Knopf, 1972.

Vento, Arnoldo C. Mestizo: *The History, Culture and Politics of the Mexican and the Chicano: The Emerging Mestizo-Americans.* Lanham, Md.: 1998.

Villar, Ernesto De Torre. *Los "Guadalupes" Y La Independencia.* Mexico City: Editorial Jus, 1966.

Weber, David J., ed. *Foreigners in their Native Land.* Albuquerque: University of New Mexico Press, 1973.

_____. *New Spain's Far Northern Frontier: Essays on Spain in the American West, 1540–1821.* Albuquerque: University of New Mexico Press, 1979.

Wolff, Paul, Barrington Moore, Jr., and Herbert Marcuse. *A Critique of Pure Tolerance.* Boston: Beacon Press, 1965.

Yoo, David K. *Growing Up Nisei: Race, Generations and Culture among Japanese Americans of California, 1924–49.* Urbana: University of Illinois Press, 2000.

WEB SITES

Gonzales, Rodolfo "Corky." "I am Joaquin/Yo Soy Joaquin." http://www.utexas.edu/students/mecha/iamjoaq.html [Accessed June 22 21:00 US/Central 2001]

"Major Authors for Children and Young Adults: Sandra Cisneros" http://www.princeton.edu/~howarth/557/house_bio.html [Accessed Wednesday August 29, 2001].

"SCHOOL IMPROVEMENT LEAGUE." The Handbook of Texas Online. http://www.tsha.utexas.edu/handbook/online/articles/view/SS/kaswm.html [Accessed Sat Jan 13 19:47:10 US/Central 2001].

Index